Air Fryer Cookbook for Beginners

Quick and Easy Preparations for Delicious, Healthy Meals from Breakfast to Dessert, including Homemade Bread Recipes

Clara Müller

© Copyright 2024 by Clara Müller - All rights reserved.

GENERAL INDEX

Introduction

Welcome to the world of air fryers! This book is specifically designed for beginners who want to learn the basics of using an air fryer. Whether you want to prepare quick everyday meals or discover healthy alternatives to traditional fried dishes, this book provides you with all the tools you need to cook effectively and with enjoyment.

Chapter 1: The Essentials of Air Fryer Technology

In this opening section, you will dive deep into the world of air fryers. Discover how these innovative kitchen appliances work and why they are an excellent addition to your kitchen setup. We explain the unique benefits that an air fryer offers, compare popular models, and show you how to find the ideal model that suits your lifestyle and cooking needs. Additionally, you will receive valuable tips on how to use your device effectively and keep it in top condition over the long term.

Introduction to Air Fryers

In the extensive market for home air fryers, selecting a model that offers high performance, practical features, and excellent value for money can be crucial for those who want to cook healthily and conveniently at home. Here is a selection of some of the best available options:

Instant Vortex Plus 6-Quart Air Fryer Oven

- **Features:** This air fryer is known for its generous capacity and user-friendly interface. It boasts powerful convection capabilities for crispy results and has a window in the basket to monitor your food easily.
- **Best For:** Overall performance, versatility, and ease of use.

Ninja Foodi DualZone XL Air Fryer

- **Features:** This model features two independent cooking zones, allowing you to cook two different foods at the same time. It also has multiple cooking functions including air fry, roast, bake, reheat, and dehydrate.
- **Best For:** Large capacity and dual-zone cooking.

Beautiful Touchscreen Air Fryer by Drew Barrymore

- **Features:** This air fryer combines style and functionality with a sleek design and a user-friendly touchscreen interface. It offers excellent performance at a budget-friendly price.
- **Best For:** Budget-conscious buyers looking for great performance.

Ninja Foodi XL Pro Air Fry Oven

- **Features:** This is a versatile air fryer toaster oven that can air fry, bake, broil, and more. It has a large capacity and comes with several useful accessories.
- **Best For:** Versatility and large capacity.

Instant Pot Duo Crisp + Air Fryer

- **Features:** This appliance combines the functionalities of a pressure cooker and an air fryer, making it extremely versatile for a variety of cooking needs. It includes multiple cooking presets and easy-to-clean parts.
- **Best For:** Multi-functionality and versatility.

These home air fryers offer high performance, practical features, and excellent value for money, making them ideal options for those looking for a solution to cook healthily and conveniently at home.

Chapter 2: Getting Started

Welcome to your new kitchen adventure with the air fryer! This chapter guides you through the basics of operating your new air fryer. From the initial setup steps to safety tips and troubleshooting, you'll learn everything necessary to use your device safely and effectively.

Unpacking and Setting Up

- **Unpacking:** Remove all packaging materials and stickers.
- **Choosing a Location:** Place the fryer on a heat-resistant, flat surface away from flammable materials.
- **Initial Cleaning:** Wash the frying basket and all removable parts with warm soapy water and dry them thoroughly before using the device for the first time.

Control Panel and Initial Settings

- **Familiarize Yourself with the Control Panel:** Get to know the buttons and settings. Most fryers have a digital display with temperature and timer functions.
- **Temperature and Timer:** Learn how to set the temperature and use the timer. Most dishes require a cooking temperature between 160°C and 200°C.
- **Preheating:** Some models require preheating, similar to a conventional oven. Check the manual to see if this is recommended for your model.

Safety Tips

- **Do Not Overfill:** Do not overfill the frying basket to ensure even cooking and to prevent the device from overheating.
- **Hot Surfaces:** Be careful when touching the device during operation, as the exterior can become very hot.
- **Automatic Shut-Off:** Use the automatic shut-off feature if your device is equipped with it to avoid overheating.

Care and Maintenance

- **Regular Cleaning:** Clean the frying basket and the interior of the device after each use.
- **Storage:** Store the fryer in a cool, dry place when not in use.
- **Technical Maintenance:** Regularly check the cord and plug for damage.

Troubleshooting

- **Device Not Heating:** Check if the device is properly plugged in and if the outlet is functioning.
- **Uneven Cooking:** Ensure that the basket is not overfilled and that the food is arranged properly for even cooking.
- **Smoke Development:** Smoke can occur if too much fat is used or if food residues burn on the heating element. Clean the device thoroughly to avoid smoke formation.

After familiarizing yourself with these basics, you are ready to use your air fryer and prepare delicious, healthy dishes quickly and easily. Enjoy cooking!

Chapter 3: Breakfast - The Energetic Start to Your Day

Start your morning in the best possible way with a selection of quick and nutritious breakfast recipes, specifically developed for preparation in the air fryer. These carefully selected recipes are not only easy to prepare but are also ideal for giving you plenty of energy to start your day. Whether savory or sweet, each dish is designed to delight your taste buds and provide your body with optimal nutrients. Discover how, with minimal preparation and quick cooking time, you can create delicious and healthy breakfast options that will enrich your daily routine.

Breakfast

Avocado-Egg Toast from the Air Fryer

PREPARATION TIME: 10 MINUTES | COOKING TIME: 10 MINUTES | PORTION SIZE: 2 SERVINGS

Ingredients:

- 2 slices of whole grain bread
- 1 ripe avocado
- 2 large eggs
- Salt and pepper, to taste
- Red pepper flakes, for garnish (optional)
- Fresh cilantro or parsley, for garnish (optional)
- Olive oil spray

Instructions:

1. Preheat the Air Fryer: Preheat your air fryer to 350°F (175°C) for about 3 minutes.
2. Prepare the Bread: Lightly spray both sides of the whole grain bread slices with olive oil spray. Place them in the air fryer basket and cook for 3-4 minutes until they are lightly toasted.
3. Prepare the Avocado: While the bread is toasting, cut the avocado in half, remove the pit, and scoop the flesh into a bowl. Mash the avocado with a fork until smooth. Season with salt and pepper to taste.
4. Cook the Eggs: Crack the eggs into small, lightly oiled ramekins or silicone molds suitable for air frying. Place them in the air fryer and cook for 6-8 minutes, or until the whites are set but the yolks are still runny.
5. Assemble the Toast: Spread the mashed avocado evenly over the toasted bread slices. Carefully remove the eggs from the ramekins and place one on each slice of avocado toast.
6. Garnish and Serve: Sprinkle with red pepper flakes and fresh cilantro or parsley if desired. Serve immediately.

NUTRITIONAL DATA: CALORIES: 350 | PROTEIN: 12G | CARBOHYDRATES: 28G | FAT: 22G | FIBER: 8G | SUGAR: 3G | SODIUM: 250MG

Banana-Nut Granola Bars

PREPARATION TIME: 15 MINUTES I COOKING TIME: 15 MINUTES I PORTION SIZE: 12 BARS

Ingredients:

- 2 cups rolled oats
- 1/2 cup chopped nuts (such as almonds, walnuts, or pecans)
- 1/2 cup mashed ripe banana (about 1 large banana)
- 1/4 cup honey or maple syrup
- 1/4 cup almond butter or peanut butter
- 1/4 cup dried fruit (such as raisins, cranberries, or apricots)
- 1/2 teaspoon vanilla extract
- 1/2 teaspoon cinnamon
- Pinch of salt

Instructions:

1. Bananen pürieren: Schälen Sie die Bananen und pürieren Sie sie in einer Schüssel mit einer Gabel oder einem Kartoffelstampfer.
2. Müslimischung vorbereiten: Fügen Sie die Haferflocken, die gehackten Nüsse, Honig, Zimt und eine Prise Salz zu den pürierten Bananen hinzu. Wenn gewünscht, können Sie jetzt auch getrocknete Früchte oder Schokoladenstückchen einrühren.
3. Masse formen: Verteilen Sie die Mischung gleichmäßig auf einem mit Backpapier ausgelegten Frittierkorb, und drücken Sie sie fest zusammen, damit die Riegel beim Backen nicht auseinanderfallen.
4. Backen in der Heißluftfritteuse: Stellen Sie den Korb in die Heißluftfritteuse und backen Sie die Mischung bei 160°C (320°F) für etwa 15 Minuten oder bis die Oberfläche fest und leicht golden ist.
5. Abkühlen und schneiden: Lassen Sie die gebackene Masse komplett abkühlen, bevor Sie sie in Riegel schneiden.

NUTRITIONAL DATA: CALORIES: 180 | PROTEIN: 4G | CARBOHYDRATES: 26G | FAT: 8G | FIBER: 3G | SUGAR: 10G | SODIUM: 60MG

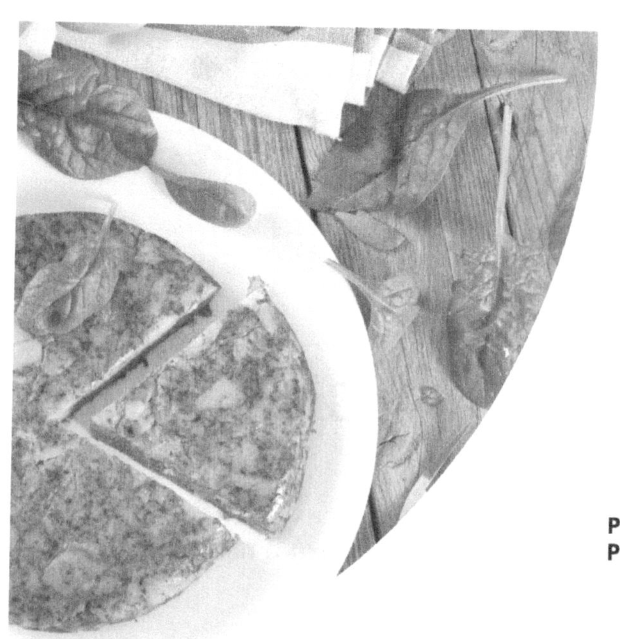

Breakfast

Sweet Potato and Spinach Frittata

PREPARATION TIME: 10 MINUTES I COOKING TIME: 20 MINUTES I PORTION SIZE: 4 SERVINGS

Ingredients:

- 1 medium sweet potato, peeled and diced
- 1 tablespoon olive oil
- 1 small onion, finely chopped
- 2 cups fresh spinach, chopped
- 6 large eggs
- 1/4 cup milk
- 1/4 cup grated Parmesan cheese
- Salt and pepper, to taste
- Cooking spray

Instructions:

1. Preheat the Air Fryer: Set your air fryer to 350°F and preheat for about 3 minutes.
2. Cook the Sweet Potato: Toss the diced sweet potato with olive oil. Place in the air fryer basket and cook for 10 minutes, shaking the basket halfway through, until tender and slightly crispy. Remove and set aside.
3. Cook the Onion and Spinach: Add the chopped onion to the air fryer basket, sprayed with a little olive oil. Cook for 3-4 minutes until translucent. Add the chopped spinach and cook for another 2-3 minutes until wilted. Remove and set aside.
4. Prepare the Egg Mixture: In a large bowl, whisk together the eggs, milk, Parmesan, salt, and pepper. Stir in the cooked sweet potato, onion, and spinach.
5. Cook the Frittata: Lightly spray a baking dish or cake pan that fits in your air fryer with cooking spray. Pour in the egg mixture and place in the air fryer basket. Cook for 10-12 minutes, or until the frittata is set and lightly browned on top.
6. Serve: Allow the frittata to cool slightly before slicing. Serve warm.

NUTRITIONAL INFORMATION: CALORIES: 180 | PROTEIN: 10G | CARBS: 12G | FAT: 10G | FIBER: 2G | SUGARS: 3G | SODIUM: 250MG

Breakfast

Almond-Berry Pancakes

PREPARATION TIME: 10 MINUTES I COOKING TIME: 8 MINUTES I PORTION SIZE: 4 SERVINGS

Ingredients:

- 1 cup almond flour
- 2 large eggs
- 1/4 cup almond milk (or any preferred milk)
- 1 tablespoon honey or maple syrup
- 1 teaspoon baking powder
- 1/2 teaspoon vanilla extract
- 1/2 cup mixed berries (blueberries, raspberries, etc.)
- Cooking spray
- Optional toppings: additional berries, maple syrup, almond butter

Instructions:

1. Preheat the Air Fryer: Preheat your air fryer to 320°F (160°C) for about 3 minutes.
2. Prepare the Batter: In a medium bowl, whisk together the almond flour, eggs, almond milk, honey (or maple syrup), baking powder, and vanilla extract until smooth. Gently fold in the mixed berries.
3. Prepare the Air Fryer Basket: Lightly spray the air fryer basket with cooking spray or line it with parchment paper.
4. Cook the Pancakes: Drop spoonfuls of the batter into the air fryer basket, forming small pancakes. Cook in batches if necessary. Air fry for 6-8 minutes, flipping halfway through, until the pancakes are golden brown and cooked through.
5. Serve: Remove the pancakes from the air fryer and serve warm with your favorite toppings, such as additional berries, maple syrup, or almond butter.

NUTRITIONAL DATA: CALORIES: 200 | PROTEIN: 8G | CARBOHYDRATES: 14G | FAT: 14G | FIBER: 4G | SUGAR: 7G | SODIUM: 180MG

Cheese-Herb-Ham Croissants

PREPARATION TIME: 15 MINUTES | COOKING TIME: 10 MINUTES | PORTION SIZE: 8 CROISSANTS

Ingredients:

- 1 can of refrigerated crescent roll dough
- 8 slices of deli ham
- 1 cup shredded cheese (cheddar, Swiss, or your favorite cheese)
- 1 tablespoon fresh herbs (such as chives, parsley, or thyme), finely chopped
- 1 egg, beaten
- Cooking spray

Instructions:

1. Preheat the Air Fryer: Preheat your air fryer to 350°F (175°C) for about 3 minutes.
2. Prepare the Dough: Unroll the crescent roll dough and separate it into 8 triangles.
3. Assemble the Croissants: Place a slice of ham on each triangle, then sprinkle with shredded cheese and chopped herbs. Roll up each triangle, starting from the wide end and rolling towards the point. Brush each croissant with the beaten egg to give it a golden, glossy finish.
4. Cook the Croissants: Lightly spray the air fryer basket with cooking spray. Place the croissants in the basket, leaving space between each one. You may need to cook in batches. Air fry for 8-10 minutes, or until the croissants are golden brown and the cheese is melted.
5. Serve: Remove the croissants from the air fryer and let them cool slightly before serving. Enjoy warm.

NUTRITIONAL DATA: CALORIES: 210 | PROTEIN: 9G | CARBOHYDRATES: 17G | FAT: 12G | FIBER: 1G | SUGAR: 4G | SODIUM: 450MG

Breakfast

Salmon Quiche with Dill and Goat Cheese

PREPARATION TIME: 15 MINUTES | COOKING TIME: 20 MINUTES | PORTION SIZE: 4 SERVINGS

Ingredients:

- 1 ready-made pie crust
- 1/2 cup cooked salmon, flaked
- 1/4 cup crumbled goat cheese
- 1/4 cup fresh dill, chopped
- 3 large eggs
- 1/2 cup milk or cream
- 1/4 teaspoon salt
- 1/4 teaspoon black pepper
- Cooking spray

Instructions:

1. Preheat the Air Fryer: Preheat your air fryer to 350°F (175°C) for about 3 minutes.
2. Prepare the Pie Crust: Lightly spray a small pie dish or quiche pan that fits in your air fryer with cooking spray. Place the ready-made pie crust into the dish, pressing it gently to fit. Trim any excess dough around the edges.
3. Add the Filling: Evenly distribute the flaked salmon, crumbled goat cheese, and chopped dill over the pie crust.
4. Mix the Egg Mixture: In a medium bowl, whisk together the eggs, milk or cream, salt, and black pepper. Pour this mixture over the salmon, cheese, and dill in the pie crust.
5. Cook the Quiche: Carefully place the pie dish in the air fryer basket. Air fry for 18-20 minutes, or until the quiche is set and the top is golden brown. If the crust begins to brown too quickly, you can reduce the temperature slightly and continue cooking until done.
6. Serve: Let the quiche cool slightly before slicing. Serve warm.

NUTRITIONAL DATA: CALORIES: 300 | PROTEIN: 14G | CARBOHYDRATES: 22G | FAT: 18G | FIBER: 1G | SUGAR: 3G | SODIUM: 450MG

Breakfast

Tomato-Basil Bruschetta on Whole Wheat Toast

PREPARATION TIME: 10 MINUTES I COOKING TIME: 8 MINUTES I PORTION SIZE: 4 SERVINGS

Ingredients:

- 4 slices whole wheat bread
- 2 cups cherry tomatoes, diced
- 1/4 cup fresh basil leaves, chopped
- 2 cloves garlic, minced
- 2 tablespoons extra-virgin olive oil
- 1 tablespoon balsamic vinegar
- Salt and pepper, to taste
- Cooking spray

Instructions:

1. Preheat the Air Fryer: Preheat your air fryer to 350°F (175°C) for about 3 minutes.
2. Prepare the Bread: Lightly spray both sides of the whole wheat bread slices with cooking spray. Place them in the air fryer basket and cook for 3-4 minutes until they are toasted and golden brown. Set aside.
3. Prepare the Tomato Mixture: In a medium bowl, combine the diced cherry tomatoes, chopped basil, minced garlic, olive oil, balsamic vinegar, salt, and pepper. Mix well to combine.
4. Assemble the Bruschetta: Spoon the tomato mixture evenly over the toasted bread slices.
5. Final Cook: Place the assembled bruschetta back in the air fryer basket and cook for an additional 2-3 minutes to warm through and meld the flavors.
6. Serve: Remove the bruschetta from the air fryer and serve immediately.

NUTRITIONAL DATA: CALORIES: 180 | PROTEIN: 5G | CARBOHYDRATES: 24G | FAT: 8G | FIBER: 4G | SUGAR: 4G | SODIUM: 220MG

Breakfast

Apple-Cinnamon Oatmeal Pies

PREPARATION TIME: 15 MINUTES I COOKING TIME: 15 MINUTES I PORTION SIZE: 6 PIES

Ingredients:

- 1 cup rolled oats
- 1/2 cup whole wheat flour
- 1/4 cup brown sugar
- 1 teaspoon ground cinnamon
- 1/4 teaspoon ground nutmeg
- 1/4 teaspoon salt
- 1/4 cup unsweetened applesauce
- 1/4 cup honey
- 1 large egg, beaten
- 1 teaspoon vanilla extract
- 1 large apple, peeled, cored, and finely chopped
- Cooking spray

Instructions:

1. Preheat the Air Fryer: Preheat your air fryer to 350°F (175°C) for about 3 minutes.
2. Prepare the Dry Ingredients: In a large bowl, mix the rolled oats, whole wheat flour, brown sugar, ground cinnamon, ground nutmeg, and salt until well combined.
3. Combine Wet Ingredients: In another bowl, whisk together the applesauce, honey, beaten egg, and vanilla extract.
4. Mix the Batter: Pour the wet ingredients into the dry ingredients and stir until just combined. Fold in the chopped apple.
5. Form the Pies: Lightly spray silicone muffin cups or small pie molds with cooking spray. Spoon the batter into the cups, filling them about two-thirds full.
6. Cook the Pies: Place the filled cups in the air fryer basket. Cook for 12-15 minutes, or until the pies are golden brown and a toothpick inserted into the center comes out clean.
7. Cool and Serve: Allow the pies to cool in the molds for a few minutes before removing. Serve warm or at room temperature.

NUTRITIONAL DATA: CALORIES: 180 | PROTEIN: 4G | CARBOHYDRATES: 36G | FAT: 2G | FIBER: 4G | SUGAR: 18G | SODIUM: 125MG

Breakfast

Herb-Mushroom Omelette

PREPARATION TIME: 10 MINUTES I COOKING TIME: 8 MINUTES I PORTION SIZE: 2 SERVINGS

Ingredients:

- 4 large eggs
- 1/2 cup mushrooms, sliced
- 1/4 cup fresh herbs (such as parsley, chives, or thyme), chopped
- 1/4 cup shredded cheese (optional)
- 1 tablespoon milk or cream
- Salt and pepper, to taste
- 1 tablespoon olive oil or melted butter
- Cooking spray

Instructions:

1. Preheat the Air Fryer: Preheat your air fryer to 350°F (175°C) for about 3 minutes.
2. Cook the Mushrooms in the Air Fryer: Toss the sliced mushrooms with olive oil or melted butter, salt, and pepper. Place the mushrooms in the air fryer basket and cook for 5-6 minutes at 350°F (175°C), shaking the basket halfway through, until the mushrooms are golden and tender.
3. Prepare the Egg Mixture: In a medium bowl, whisk together the eggs, milk or cream, salt, and pepper. Stir in the fresh herbs and cooked mushrooms. Add the shredded cheese if desired.
4. Cook the Omelette: Lightly spray a small oven-safe dish or cake pan that fits in your air fryer with cooking spray. Pour the egg mixture into the dish and place it in the air fryer basket. Cook for 6-8 minutes, or until the omelette is set and slightly golden on top.
5. Serve: Remove the omelette from the air fryer, slice it, and serve immediately.

NUTRITIONAL DATA: CALORIES: 210 | PROTEIN: 15G | CARBOHYDRATES: 4G | FAT: 15G | FIBER: 1G | SUGAR: 2G | SODIUM: 200MG

Breakfast

Pear-Walnut Crisp

PREPARATION TIME: 10 MINUTES I COOKING TIME: 10 MINUTES I PORTION SIZE: 2 SERVINGS

Ingredients:

- 3 ripe pears, peeled, cored, and sliced
- 1/2 cup rolled oats
- 1/4 cup chopped walnuts
- 1/4 cup brown sugar
- 1/4 cup all-purpose flour
- 1/2 teaspoon ground cinnamon
- 1/4 teaspoon ground nutmeg
- 3 tablespoons butter, melted
- 1 tablespoon honey or maple syrup
- Cooking spray

Instructions:

1. Preheat the Air Fryer: Preheat your air fryer to 350°F (175°C) for about 3 minutes.
2. Prepare the Pear Filling: In a medium bowl, toss the sliced pears with 1 tablespoon of honey or maple syrup and a pinch of cinnamon. Set aside.
3. Prepare the Crisp Topping: In a separate bowl, combine the rolled oats, chopped walnuts, brown sugar, flour, ground cinnamon, ground nutmeg, and melted butter. Mix until the ingredients are well combined and crumbly.
4. Assemble the Crisp: Lightly spray a small oven-safe dish or cake pan that fits in your air fryer with cooking spray. Spread the pear mixture evenly in the dish, then sprinkle the crisp topping over the pears.
5. Cook the Crisp: Place the dish in the air fryer basket and cook for 12-15 minutes, or until the topping is golden brown and the pears are tender.
6. Serve: Let the pear-walnut crisp cool slightly before serving. Enjoy it warm, possibly with a scoop of vanilla ice cream or a dollop of whipped cream.

NUTRITIONAL DATA: CALORIES: 280 | PROTEIN: 3G | CARBOHYDRATES: 40G | FAT: 14G | FIBER: 5G | SUGAR: 24G | SODIUM: 45MG

Chapter 4: Main Courses - Variety and Flavor from the Air Fryer

Unlock the full potential of your air fryer with a wide range of main course recipes that are both flavorful and healthy. This chapter offers a variety of recipes, from succulent meat and tender fish dishes to delicious vegetarian creations. Each dish has been carefully selected to highlight the flavors of the ingredients while minimizing fat content. Discover how simple and efficient it is to prepare wholesome meals for yourself and your family that are not only healthy but also rich in flavors. Get inspired and bring variety to your menu with dishes that are quick to prepare and satisfy every taste.

Lunch and Dinner with Meat

Rustic Herb-Crusted Pork Roast
Lemon-Rosemary Chicken Thighs
Entrecôte with Garlic Butter
Spicy Lamb Chops with Mint Pesto
Pepper Steak with Mushroom Sauce
Thyme Beef Skewers
Parmesan-Herb Crusted Chicken Breast
Duck Breast with Sweet Potato Puree
Wiener Schnitzel from the Air Fryer
Veal Medallions in Dijon Mustard Sauce
Tuscan Meatballs with Sun-Dried Tomatoes
Bell Pepper Beef with Onions
Beer Marinated Chicken Drumsticks
Beef Meatballs with Feta and Olives
Turkey Breast with Cranberry Glaze

Lunch and Dinner with Fish

Cod Fillets with Lemon Herb Crust
Salmon Steaks with Honey Mustard Glaze
Trout Packets with Dill and White Wine
Cod in Lemon Dill Sauce
Shrimp Skewers with Garlic and Chili
Sole in Almond Butter
Halibut Fillet with Basil Pesto
Calamari Rings with Aioli Dip
Flounder Fillets with Tomato Olive Salsa
Sea Bream in Paprika Crust
Sea Bass with Herb Crust
Cod with Sesame Ginger Glaze
Salmon Fillet with Herb Crust
Tuna Steaks with Lemon Caper Sauce
Fish with Bell Pepper Vegetables

Vegetarian and Vegan Lunch and Dinner

Stuffed Eggplants with Quinoa and Pine Nuts
Sweet Potato Chickpea Burgers
Vegan Lentil Stew with Coconut Milk
Beet Risotto with Walnuts
Zucchini Lasagna
Braised Tofu in Ginger Tomato Sauce
Mushroom and Spinach Strudel
Potato Gnocchi with Tomato Basil Sauce
Roasted Cauliflower with Turmeric and Almonds
Savory Vegetable and Cheese Tart
Spinach and Feta Savory Pie
Balsamic-Glazed Carrots with Thyme
Kale Chips with Sea Salt and Lemon
Pumpkin Quinoa Fritters
Eggplant Rolls Stuffed with Vegan Ricotta and Spinach

Lunch and Dinner with Meat

Rustic Herb-Crusted Pork Roast

PREPARATION TIME: 15 MINUTES | COOKING TIME: 45 MINUTES | PORTION SIZE: 4 SERVINGS

Ingredients:

- 2 lbs pork loin roast
- 2 tablespoons olive oil
- 3 cloves garlic, minced
- 1 tablespoon fresh rosemary, chopped
- 1 tablespoon fresh thyme, chopped
- 1 teaspoon dried oregano
- 1 teaspoon sea salt
- 1/2 teaspoon black pepper
- Cooking spray

Instructions:

1. Preheat the Air Fryer: Set your air fryer to 375°F (190°C) and preheat for about 3 minutes.
2. Prepare the Herb Mixture: In a small bowl, mix together the minced garlic, rosemary, thyme, oregano, salt, and black pepper. Add the olive oil and stir to create a paste.
3. Season the Pork: Rub the herb mixture evenly over the pork loin roast, pressing it onto the meat to create a crust.
4. Cook the Pork Roast: Lightly spray the air fryer basket with cooking spray. Place the pork roast into the basket and cook for 20 minutes. After 20 minutes, reduce the temperature to 350°F (175°C) and continue cooking for an additional 25 minutes, or until the internal temperature reaches 145°F (63°C).
5. Rest and Serve: Remove the pork roast from the air fryer and let it rest for 10 minutes before slicing. Serve warm.

NUTRITIONAL DATA: CALORIES: 350 | PROTEIN: 32G | CARBOHYDRATES: 1G | FAT: 23G | FIBER: 0G | SUGAR: 0G | SODIUM: 600MG

Lunch and Dinner with Meat

Lemon-Rosemary Chicken Thighs

PREPARATION TIME: 10 MINUTES I COOKING TIME: 25 MINUTES I PORTION SIZE: 4 SERVINGS

Ingredients:

- 4 bone-in, skin-on chicken thighs
- 2 tablespoons olive oil
- Juice of 1 lemon
- Zest of 1 lemon
- 2 tablespoons fresh rosemary, chopped
- 3 cloves garlic, minced
- 1 teaspoon sea salt
- 1/2 teaspoon black pepper
- Cooking spray

Instructions:

1. Preheat the Air Fryer: Set your air fryer to 375°F (190°C) and preheat for about 3 minutes.
2. Prepare the Marinade: In a small bowl, whisk together the olive oil, lemon juice, lemon zest, chopped rosemary, minced garlic, salt, and black pepper.
3. Marinate the Chicken: Pat the chicken thighs dry with paper towels. Rub the lemon-rosemary mixture evenly over the chicken thighs, ensuring the marinade coats the skin well.
4. Cook the Chicken Thighs: Lightly spray the air fryer basket with cooking spray. Place the chicken thighs skin-side down in the basket and cook for 12 minutes. Flip the thighs and cook for an additional 13 minutes, or until the internal temperature reaches 165°F (74°C) and the skin is crispy and golden brown.
5. Serve: Remove the chicken from the air fryer and let it rest for a few minutes before serving. Garnish with additional rosemary if desired.

NUTRITIONAL DATA: CALORIES: 320 | PROTEIN: 24G | CARBOHYDRATES: 1G | FAT: 24G | FIBER: 0G | SUGAR: 0G | SODIUM: 500MG

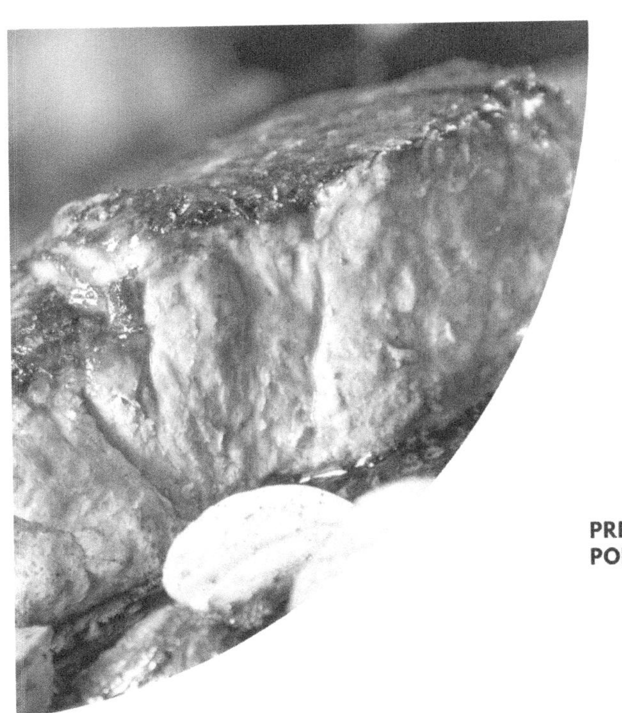

Entrecôte with Garlic Butter

PREPARATION TIME: 10 MINUTES | COOKING TIME: 12 MINUTES | PORTION SIZE: 2 SERVINGS

Ingredients:

- 2 entrecôte steaks (about 8 oz each)
- 2 tablespoons unsalted butter, softened
- 3 cloves garlic, minced
- 1 tablespoon fresh parsley, chopped
- 1 teaspoon fresh thyme, chopped
- 1 tablespoon olive oil
- Salt and pepper, to taste
- Cooking spray

Instructions:

1. Preheat the Air Fryer: Set your air fryer to 400°F (200°C) and preheat for about 3 minutes.
2. Prepare the Garlic Butter: In a small bowl, mix together the softened butter, minced garlic, chopped parsley, and thyme. Set aside.
3. Season the Steaks: Pat the entrecôte steaks dry with paper towels. Rub the steaks with olive oil, then season generously with salt and pepper on both sides.
4. Cook the Steaks: Lightly spray the air fryer basket with cooking spray. Place the steaks in the basket in a single layer, making sure they do not overlap. Cook for 6 minutes on one side, then flip the steaks and cook for another 4-6 minutes, depending on your desired level of doneness (medium-rare is usually reached at an internal temperature of 130°F/54°C).
5. Rest and Serve: Remove the steaks from the air fryer and let them rest for 5 minutes. Just before serving, top each steak with a dollop of the garlic butter, allowing it to melt over the meat.

NUTRITIONAL DATA: CALORIES: 450 | PROTEIN: 35G | CARBOHYDRATES: 1G | FAT: 34G | FIBER: 0G | SUGAR: 0G | SODIUM: 400MG

Lunch and Dinner with Meat

Spicy Lamb Chops with Mint Pesto

PREPARATION TIME: 15 MINUTES I COOKING TIME: 12 MINUTES I PORTION SIZE: 4 SERVINGS

Ingredients:

- For the Lamb Chops:
- 8 lamb chops (about 1 inch thick)
- 2 tablespoons olive oil
- 2 cloves garlic, minced
- 1 teaspoon ground cumin
- 1 teaspoon ground coriander
- 1/2 teaspoon cayenne pepper
- 1 teaspoon salt
- 1/2 teaspoon black pepper
- For the Mint Pesto:
- 1 cup fresh mint leaves
- 1/4 cup fresh parsley leaves
- 1/4 cup pine nuts or almonds
- 1/2 cup olive oil
- 1/4 cup grated Parmesan cheese
- 2 cloves garlic, minced
- Juice of 1 lemon
- Salt and pepper, to taste

Instructions:

1. Preheat the Air Fryer: Set your air fryer to 400°F (200°C) and preheat for about 3 minutes.
2. Season the Lamb Chops: In a small bowl, mix together the olive oil, minced garlic, ground cumin, ground coriander, cayenne pepper, salt, and black pepper. Rub this mixture evenly over the lamb chops, ensuring they are well coated.
3. Cook the Lamb Chops: Lightly spray the air fryer basket with cooking spray. Place the lamb chops in the basket in a single layer. Cook for 6 minutes, then flip and cook for an additional 6 minutes, or until the internal temperature reaches 145°F (63°C) for medium-rare.
4. Prepare the Mint Pesto: While the lamb chops are cooking, prepare the mint pesto. In a food processor, combine the mint leaves, parsley, pine nuts (or almonds), olive oil, Parmesan cheese, minced garlic, and lemon juice. Blend until smooth. Season with salt and pepper to taste.
5. Serve: Remove the lamb chops from the air fryer and let them rest for a few minutes. Serve warm with a generous spoonful of mint pesto on top.

NUTRITIONAL DATA: CALORIES: 520 | PROTEIN: 34G | CARBOHYDRATES: 3G | FAT: 42G | FIBER: 1G | SUGAR: 1G | SODIUM: 600MG

Pepper Steak with Mushroom Sauce

PREPARATION TIME: 15 MINUTES | COOKING TIME: 20 MINUTES | PORTION SIZE: 4 SERVINGS

Ingredients:

For the Pepper Steak:

- 4 beef steaks (about 6 oz each, such as sirloin or ribeye)
- 2 tablespoons olive oil
- 1 tablespoon freshly ground black pepper
- 1 teaspoon salt

For the Mushroom Sauce:

- 2 cups mushrooms, sliced
- 1 tablespoon butter
- 1 tablespoon olive oil
- 1/2 cup beef broth
- 1/4 cup cream
- 2 garlic cloves, minced
- Salt and pepper, to taste
- Cooking spray

Instructions:

1. Preheat the Air Fryer to 350°F (180°C) for 3 minutes.
2. Prepare the Mushroom Sauce: Cook the sliced mushrooms in a small oven-safe dish or foil in the air fryer. Add butter and olive oil and air fry for 5-7 minutes until golden and tender.
3. Finish the Sauce: Add garlic, beef broth, and cream to the mushrooms. Stir well and cook for an additional 3-4 minutes until thickened. Season with salt and pepper. Keep warm.
4. Preheat Again: Set the air fryer to 400°F (200°C) and preheat for another 3 minutes.
5. Season the Steaks: Pat steaks dry, rub with olive oil, and season with salt and freshly ground black pepper.
6. Cook the Steaks: Lightly spray the air fryer basket with cooking spray. Place steaks in a single layer and cook for 10-12 minutes, flipping halfway, until the desired doneness is reached (130°F/54°C for medium-rare).
7. Serve: Pour the warm mushroom sauce over the rested steaks and serve immediately.

NUTRITIONAL DATA: CALORIES: 450 | PROTEIN: 34G | CARBOHYDRATES: 6G | FAT: 32G | FIBER: 1G | SUGAR: 1G | SODIUM: 600MG

Lunch and Dinner with Meat

Thyme Beef Skewers

PREPARATION TIME: 10 MINUTES I COOKING TIME: 10 MINUTES I PORTION SIZE: 4 SERVINGS

Ingredients:

- 1 lb beef sirloin, cut into 1-inch cubes
- 2 tablespoons olive oil
- 2 tablespoons fresh thyme leaves, chopped
- 2 cloves garlic, minced
- 1 teaspoon salt
- 1/2 teaspoon black pepper
- 1 red bell pepper, cut into 1-inch pieces
- 1 yellow bell pepper, cut into 1-inch pieces
- 1 red onion, cut into wedges
- Cooking spray

Instructions:

1. Preheat the Air Fryer: Set your air fryer to 400°F (200°C) and preheat for about 3 minutes.
2. Marinate the Beef: In a large bowl, combine the olive oil, chopped thyme, minced garlic, salt, and black pepper. Add the beef cubes and toss to coat. Let marinate for at least 10 minutes.
3. Assemble the Skewers: Thread the marinated beef cubes onto skewers, alternating with pieces of red bell pepper, yellow bell pepper, and red onion.
4. Cook the Skewers: Lightly spray the air fryer basket with cooking spray. Place the skewers in the basket in a single layer. Cook for 8-10 minutes, turning halfway through, until the beef is cooked to your desired level of doneness.
5. Serve: Remove the skewers from the air fryer and serve hot.

NUTRITIONAL DATA: CALORIES: 290 | PROTEIN: 26G | CARBOHYDRATES: 8G | FAT: 18G | FIBER: 2G | SUGAR: 4G | SODIUM: 500MG

Parmesan-Herb Crusted Chicken Breast

PREPARATION TIME: 10 MINUTES I COOKING TIME: 15 MINUTES I PORTION SIZE: 4 SERVINGS

Ingredients:

- 4 boneless, skinless chicken breasts
- 1/2 cup grated Parmesan cheese
- 1/4 cup breadcrumbs (optional for extra crispiness)
- 2 tablespoons fresh parsley, chopped
- 1 tablespoon fresh thyme, chopped
- 1 tablespoon fresh rosemary, chopped
- 2 cloves garlic, minced
- 2 tablespoons olive oil
- 1/2 teaspoon salt
- 1/4 teaspoon black pepper
- Cooking spray

Instructions:

1. Preheat the Air Fryer: Set your air fryer to 375°F (190°C) and preheat for about 3 minutes.
2. Prepare the Herb Crust: In a small bowl, mix together the grated Parmesan cheese, breadcrumbs (if using), chopped parsley, thyme, rosemary, minced garlic, salt, and black pepper.
3. Coat the Chicken: Brush the chicken breasts with olive oil, then press each breast into the Parmesan-herb mixture, coating both sides evenly.
4. Cook the Chicken: Lightly spray the air fryer basket with cooking spray. Place the chicken breasts in the basket in a single layer. Cook for 12-15 minutes, flipping halfway through, until the chicken is golden brown and the internal temperature reaches 165°F (74°C).
5. Serve: Remove the chicken from the air fryer and let it rest for a few minutes before serving.

NUTRITIONAL DATA: CALORIES: 320 | PROTEIN: 40G | CARBOHYDRATES: 3G | FAT: 16G | FIBER: 1G | SUGAR: 0G | SODIUM: 600MG

Lunch and Dinner with Meat

Duck Breast with Sweet Potato Puree

PREPARATION TIME: 15 MINUTES I COOKING TIME: 25 MINUTES I PORTION SIZE: 2 SERVINGS

Ingredients:

- For the Duck Breast:
- 2 duck breasts, skin on
- 1 teaspoon sea salt
- 1/2 teaspoon black pepper
- 1 teaspoon fresh thyme leaves, chopped
- 1 tablespoon olive oil
- For the Sweet Potato Puree:
- 2 medium sweet potatoes, peeled and diced
- 2 tablespoons unsalted butter
- 1/4 cup milk or cream
- Salt and pepper, to taste
- Cooking spray

Instructions:

1. Preheat the Air Fryer: Set your air fryer to 375°F (190°C) and preheat for about 3 minutes.
2. Prepare the Duck Breasts: Score the skin of the duck breasts in a crisscross pattern, being careful not to cut into the meat. Rub the duck breasts with olive oil, salt, pepper, and chopped thyme.
3. Cook the Duck Breasts: Place the duck breasts skin-side down in the air fryer basket. Cook for 12 minutes at 375°F, then flip and cook for an additional 8-10 minutes, or until the internal temperature reaches 135°F (57°C) for medium-rare. Let the duck rest for 5 minutes before slicing.
4. Prepare the Sweet Potato Puree: While the duck is cooking, toss the diced sweet potatoes with a little cooking spray. Place them in the air fryer basket and cook for 12-15 minutes at 375°F, shaking the basket halfway through, until the potatoes are tender.
5. Make the Puree: Transfer the cooked sweet potatoes to a bowl. Add the butter, milk or cream, salt, and pepper, then mash until smooth and creamy.
6. Serve: Slice the duck breast and serve it over the sweet potato puree.

NUTRITIONAL DATA: CALORIES: 550 | PROTEIN: 35G | CARBOHYDRATES: 35G | FAT: 30G | FIBER: 6G | SUGAR: 9G | SODIUM: 600MG

Wiener Schnitzel from the Air Fryer

PREPARATION TIME: 10 MINUTES | COOKING TIME: 12 MINUTES | PORTION SIZE: 4 SERVINGS

Ingredients:

- 4 veal cutlets, about 1/4 inch thick
- 1/2 cup all-purpose flour
- 2 large eggs, beaten
- 1 cup breadcrumbs (preferably fresh)
- 1 teaspoon salt
- 1/2 teaspoon black pepper
- Lemon wedges, for serving
- Cooking spray

Instructions:

1. Preheat the Air Fryer: Set your air fryer to 400°F (200°C) and preheat for about 3 minutes.
2. Prepare the Schnitzel: Season the veal cutlets with salt and pepper on both sides. Dredge each cutlet in flour, shaking off any excess. Dip in the beaten eggs, then coat thoroughly with breadcrumbs, pressing gently to adhere.
3. Cook the Schnitzel: Lightly spray the air fryer basket with cooking spray. Place the breaded cutlets in the basket in a single layer. Lightly spray the tops with cooking spray as well. Air fry for 10-12 minutes, flipping halfway through, until the schnitzels are golden brown and crispy.
4. Serve: Serve the Wiener Schnitzel hot, garnished with lemon wedges.

NUTRITIONAL DATA: CALORIES: 350 | PROTEIN: 30G | CARBOHYDRATES: 25G | FAT: 15G | FIBER: 2G | SUGAR: 1G | SODIUM: 700MG

Lunch and Dinner with Meat

Veal Medallions in Dijon Mustard Sauce

PREPARATION TIME: 10 MINUTES | COOKING TIME: 15 MINUTES | PORTION SIZE: 4 SERVINGS

Ingredients:

- 4 veal medallions (about 4 oz each)
- 2 tablespoons Dijon mustard
- 1/2 cup heavy cream
- 1/4 cup chicken or beef broth
- 2 tablespoons olive oil
- 2 cloves garlic, minced
- 1 tablespoon fresh parsley, chopped (optional)
- Salt and pepper, to taste
- Cooking spray

Instructions:

1. Preheat the Air Fryer: Set your air fryer to 375°F (190°C) and preheat for about 3 minutes.
2. Prepare the Veal Medallions: Pat the veal medallions dry with paper towels. Season both sides with salt and pepper. Brush each medallion with olive oil.
3. Cook the Veal Medallions: Lightly spray the air fryer basket with cooking spray. Place the veal medallions in the basket in a single layer. Air fry for 8-10 minutes, flipping halfway through, until the medallions are golden brown and cooked to your desired doneness (145°F/63°C for medium).
4. Prepare the Dijon Mustard Sauce: While the veal is cooking, heat a small pan on the stovetop over medium heat. Add the minced garlic and sauté for 1-2 minutes until fragrant. Stir in the Dijon mustard, heavy cream, and broth. Bring the mixture to a simmer and cook for 3-4 minutes until the sauce has thickened. Season with salt and pepper to taste.
5. Serve: Pour the Dijon mustard sauce over the cooked veal medallions. Garnish with fresh parsley if desired. Serve immediately.

NUTRITIONAL DATA: CALORIES: 400 | PROTEIN: 28G | CARBOHYDRATES: 2G | FAT: 30G | FIBER: 0G | SUGAR: 1G | SODIUM: 600MG

Lunch and Dinner with Meat

Tuscan Meatballs with Sun-Dried Tomatoes

PREPARATION TIME: 15 MINUTES I COOKING TIME: 12 MINUTES I PORTION SIZE: 4 SERVINGS

Ingredients:

- 1 lb ground beef or a mix of beef and pork
- 1/2 cup breadcrumbs
- 1/4 cup sun-dried tomatoes, finely chopped
- 1/4 cup grated Parmesan cheese
- 2 cloves garlic, minced
- 1 large egg
- 2 tablespoons fresh parsley, chopped
- 1 tablespoon fresh basil, chopped
- 1 teaspoon dried oregano
- 1/2 teaspoon salt
- 1/4 teaspoon black pepper
- Cooking spray

Instructions:

1. Preheat the Air Fryer: Set your air fryer to 375°F (190°C) and preheat for about 3 minutes.
2. Prepare the Meatballs: In a large bowl, combine the ground meat, breadcrumbs, sun-dried tomatoes, Parmesan cheese, minced garlic, egg, parsley, basil, oregano, salt, and black pepper. Mix until all ingredients are well combined.
3. Form the Meatballs: Roll the mixture into 1-inch meatballs. Lightly spray the air fryer basket with cooking spray and place the meatballs in the basket in a single layer.
4. Cook the Meatballs: Air fry the meatballs for 10-12 minutes, shaking the basket halfway through, until the meatballs are browned and cooked through.
5. Serve: Serve the Tuscan meatballs warm, garnished with additional fresh herbs if desired. They can be served on their own, with pasta, or as part of a larger meal.

NUTRITIONAL DATA: CALORIES: 350 | PROTEIN: 24G | CARBOHYDRATES: 10G | FAT: 24G | FIBER: 2G | SUGAR: 2G | SODIUM: 600MG

Lunch and Dinner with Meat

Bell Pepper Beef with Onions

PREPARATION TIME: 10 MINUTES I COOKING TIME: 15 MINUTES I PORTION SIZE: 4 SERVINGS

Ingredients:

- 1 lb beef sirloin, thinly sliced
- 2 bell peppers (red and yellow), sliced into strips
- 1 large onion, sliced
- 2 tablespoons soy sauce
- 1 tablespoon olive oil
- 1 tablespoon cornstarch
- 2 cloves garlic, minced
- 1 teaspoon ground black pepper
- 1/2 teaspoon salt
- 1 teaspoon sesame oil (optional)
- Cooking spray

Instructions:

1. Preheat the Air Fryer: Set your air fryer to 400°F (200°C) and preheat for about 3 minutes.
2. Marinate the Beef: In a bowl, mix the sliced beef with soy sauce, olive oil, cornstarch, minced garlic, black pepper, and salt. Let it marinate for 10 minutes while you prepare the vegetables.
3. Prepare the Vegetables: Toss the bell pepper strips and onion slices with a little cooking spray to coat them lightly.
4. Cook the Beef: Place the marinated beef in the air fryer basket in a single layer. Cook for 8-10 minutes, shaking the basket halfway through, until the beef is browned and cooked through.
5. Cook the Vegetables: Add the bell peppers and onions to the air fryer basket with the cooked beef. Cook for an additional 5 minutes until the vegetables are tender and slightly charred.
6. Serve: Drizzle with sesame oil if desired and serve the bell pepper beef with onions hot.

NUTRITIONAL DATA: CALORIES: 320 | PROTEIN: 25G | CARBOHYDRATES: 10G | FAT: 20G | FIBER: 3G | SUGAR: 5G | SODIUM: 700MG

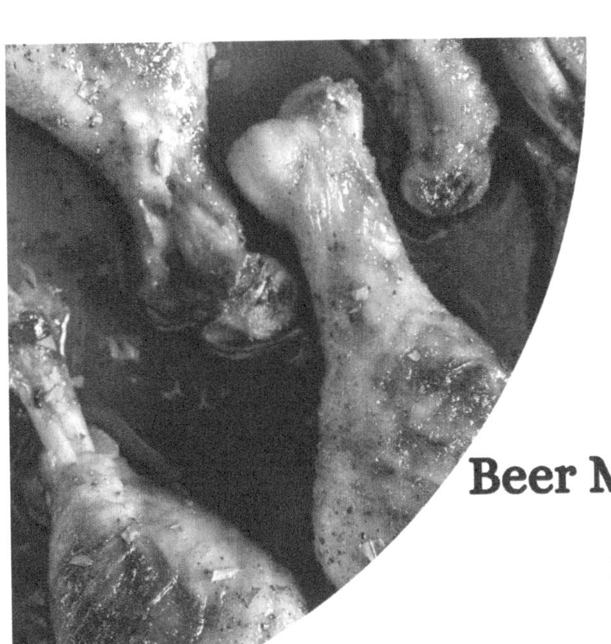

Lunch and Dinner with Meat

Beer Marinated Chicken Drumsticks

PREPARATION TIME: 10 MINUTES | COOKING TIME: 25 MINUTES | PORTION SIZE: 4 SERVINGS

Ingredients:

- 8 chicken drumsticks
- 1 cup beer (lager or pale ale works well)
- 2 tablespoons olive oil
- 2 cloves garlic, minced
- 1 teaspoon paprika
- 1 teaspoon dried oregano
- 1 teaspoon salt
- 1/2 teaspoon black pepper
- 1 tablespoon honey (optional)
- Cooking spray

Instructions:

1. Preheat the Air Fryer: Set your air fryer to 375°F (190°C) and preheat for about 3 minutes.
2. Marinate the Chicken: In a large bowl, mix together the beer, olive oil, minced garlic, paprika, oregano, salt, black pepper, and honey if using. Add the chicken drumsticks, ensuring they are fully coated in the marinade. Let them marinate in the refrigerator for at least 30 minutes, or up to 4 hours for best results.
3. Cook the Drumsticks: Lightly spray the air fryer basket with cooking spray. Remove the chicken drumsticks from the marinade, allowing excess marinade to drip off, and place them in the air fryer basket in a single layer. Cook for 20-25 minutes, turning halfway through, until the chicken is cooked through and the skin is crispy. The internal temperature should reach 165°F (74°C).
4. Serve: Serve the beer marinated chicken drumsticks hot, with your favorite side dishes.

NUTRITIONAL DATA: CALORIES: 280 | PROTEIN: 25G | CARBOHYDRATES: 5G | FAT: 18G | FIBER: 0G | SUGAR: 1G | SODIUM: 600MG

Lunch and Dinner with Meat

Beef Meatballs with Feta and Olives

PREPARATION TIME: 15 MINUTES I COOKING TIME: 12 MINUTES I PORTION SIZE: 4 SERVINGS

Ingredients:

- 1 lb ground beef
- 1/2 cup crumbled feta cheese
- 1/4 cup pitted black olives, chopped
- 1/4 cup breadcrumbs
- 1 egg, beaten
- 2 cloves garlic, minced
- 1 tablespoon fresh parsley, chopped
- 1 teaspoon dried oregano
- 1/2 teaspoon salt
- 1/4 teaspoon black pepper
- Cooking spray

Instructions:

1. Preheat the Air Fryer: Set your air fryer to 375°F (190°C) and preheat for about 3 minutes.
2. Prepare the Meatballs: In a large bowl, combine the ground beef, crumbled feta, chopped olives, breadcrumbs, beaten egg, minced garlic, parsley, oregano, salt, and black pepper. Mix until well combined.
3. Form the Meatballs: Shape the mixture into 1-inch meatballs. Lightly spray the air fryer basket with cooking spray and place the meatballs in the basket in a single layer.
4. Cook the Meatballs: Air fry the meatballs for 10-12 minutes, shaking the basket halfway through cooking, until the meatballs are browned and cooked through.
5. Serve: Serve the meatballs hot, either as an appetizer or as part of a main dish.

NUTRITIONAL DATA: CALORIES: 310 | PROTEIN: 22G | CARBOHYDRATES: 4G | FAT: 23G | FIBER: 1G | SUGAR: 1G | SODIUM: 700MG

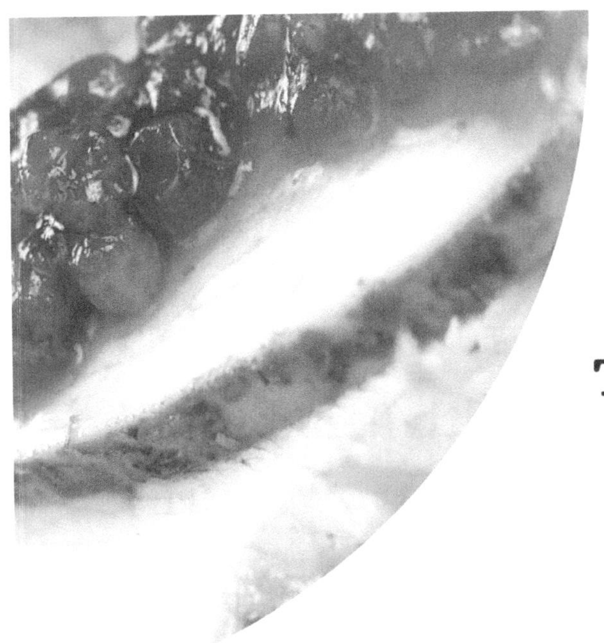

Lunch and Dinner with Meat

Turkey Breast with Cranberry Glaze

PREPARATION TIME: 10 MINUTES | COOKING TIME: 25 MINUTES | PORTION SIZE: 4 SERVINGS

Ingredients:

- 1.5 lbs turkey breast, boneless and skinless
- 1/2 cup cranberry sauce (homemade or store-bought)
- 2 tablespoons honey
- 1 tablespoon Dijon mustard
- 1 tablespoon olive oil
- 2 cloves garlic, minced
- 1 teaspoon fresh rosemary, chopped
- 1/2 teaspoon salt
- 1/4 teaspoon black pepper
- Cooking spray

Instructions:

1. Preheat the Air Fryer: Set your air fryer to 375°F (190°C) and preheat for about 3 minutes.
2. Prepare the Cranberry Glaze: In a small bowl, mix together the cranberry sauce, honey, Dijon mustard, minced garlic, chopped rosemary, salt, and pepper.
3. Season the Turkey: Rub the turkey breast with olive oil and season lightly with additional salt and pepper. Brush half of the cranberry glaze over the turkey breast.
4. Cook the Turkey: Lightly spray the air fryer basket with cooking spray. Place the turkey breast in the air fryer basket and cook for 20-25 minutes, flipping halfway through and brushing with the remaining glaze. Cook until the internal temperature reaches 165°F (74°C).
5. Serve: Allow the turkey breast to rest for 5 minutes before slicing. Serve warm with any extra glaze drizzled over the top.

NUTRITIONAL DATA: CALORIES: 280 | PROTEIN: 32G | CARBOHYDRATES: 15G | FAT: 10G | FIBER: 1G | SUGAR: 13G | SODIUM: 450MG

Lunch and Dinner with Fish

Cod Fillets with Lemon Herb Crust

PREPARATION TIME: 10 MINUTES I COOKING TIME: 12 MINUTES I PORTION SIZE: 4 SERVINGS

Ingredients:

- 4 cod fillets (about 6 oz each)
- 1/2 cup breadcrumbs (preferably panko)
- 1/4 cup grated Parmesan cheese
- Zest of 1 lemon
- 2 tablespoons fresh parsley, chopped
- 1 tablespoon fresh dill, chopped
- 2 cloves garlic, minced
- 2 tablespoons olive oil
- Salt and pepper, to taste
- Cooking spray
- Lemon wedges, for serving

Instructions:

1. Preheat the Air Fryer: Set your air fryer to 400°F (200°C) and preheat for about 3 minutes.
2. Prepare the Lemon Herb Crust: In a small bowl, combine the breadcrumbs, grated Parmesan cheese, lemon zest, chopped parsley, chopped dill, minced garlic, salt, and pepper. Stir in the olive oil until the mixture is well combined and resembles wet sand.
3. Coat the Cod Fillets: Pat the cod fillets dry with paper towels. Season both sides with salt and pepper. Press the breadcrumb mixture onto the top of each fillet, ensuring it adheres well.
4. Cook the Cod Fillets: Lightly spray the air fryer basket with cooking spray. Place the fillets in the basket, crust-side up, in a single layer. Air fry for 10-12 minutes, or until the crust is golden brown and the fish is cooked through (it should flake easily with a fork).
5. Serve: Serve the cod fillets hot, with lemon wedges on the side for squeezing over the top.

NUTRITIONAL DATA: CALORIES: 280 | PROTEIN: 25G | CARBOHYDRATES: 10G | FAT: 15G | FIBER: 1G | SUGAR: 1G | SODIUM: 450MG

Lunch and Dinner with Fish

Salmon Steaks with Honey Mustard Glaze

PREPARATION TIME: 10 MINUTES | COOKING TIME: 10 MINUTES | PORTION SIZE: 4 SERVINGS

Ingredients:

- 4 salmon steaks (about 6 oz each)
- 2 tablespoons honey
- 1 tablespoon Dijon mustard
- 1 tablespoon whole-grain mustard
- 1 tablespoon olive oil
- 1 tablespoon lemon juice
- 2 cloves garlic, minced
- Salt and pepper, to taste
- Cooking spray
- Fresh dill, for garnish (optional)

Instructions:

1. Preheat the Air Fryer: Set your air fryer to 400°F (200°C) and preheat for about 3 minutes.
2. Prepare the Honey Mustard Glaze: In a small bowl, whisk together the honey, Dijon mustard, whole-grain mustard, olive oil, lemon juice, minced garlic, salt, and pepper.
3. Season the Salmon Steaks: Pat the salmon steaks dry with paper towels. Brush both sides of each steak with the honey mustard glaze.
4. Cook the Salmon: Lightly spray the air fryer basket with cooking spray. Place the salmon steaks in the basket in a single layer. Cook for 8-10 minutes, flipping halfway through, until the salmon is cooked through and flakes easily with a fork.
5. Serve: Garnish the salmon steaks with fresh dill if desired. Serve hot with your favorite sides.

NUTRITIONAL DATA: CALORIES: 350 | PROTEIN: 30G | CARBOHYDRATES: 10G | FAT: 20G | FIBER: 0G | SUGAR: 8G | SODIUM: 400MG

Trout Packets with Dill and White Wine

PREPARATION TIME: 10 MINUTES I COOKING TIME: 15 MINUTES I PORTION SIZE: 4 SERVINGS

Ingredients:

- 4 trout fillets (about 6 oz each)
- 1/4 cup dry white wine
- 2 tablespoons fresh dill, chopped
- 2 tablespoons unsalted butter, melted
- 1 lemon, thinly sliced
- 2 cloves garlic, minced
- Salt and pepper, to taste
- Cooking spray

Instructions:

1. Preheat the Air Fryer: Set your air fryer to 375°F (190°C) and preheat for about 3 minutes.
2. Prepare the Trout Packets: Cut four pieces of parchment paper or aluminum foil large enough to wrap the trout fillets. Place a trout fillet in the center of each piece. Drizzle with melted butter and white wine, then sprinkle with chopped dill and minced garlic. Top each fillet with lemon slices and season with salt and pepper.
3. Seal the Packets: Fold the parchment or foil over the trout fillets to create sealed packets.
4. Cook the Trout: Place the packets in the air fryer basket in a single layer. Cook for 12-15 minutes, or until the trout is cooked through and flakes easily with a fork.
5. Serve: Carefully open the packets and serve the trout with the juices and lemon slices.

NUTRITIONAL DATA: CALORIES: 280 | PROTEIN: 25G | CARBOHYDRATES: 3G | FAT: 18G | FIBER: 0G | SUGAR: 0G | SODIUM: 300MG

Cod in Lemon Dill Sauce

PREPARATION TIME: 10 MINUTES | COOKING TIME: 12 MINUTES | PORTION SIZE: 4 SERVINGS

Ingredients:

- 4 trout fillets (about 6 oz each)
- 1/4 cup dry white wine
- 2 tablespoons fresh dill, chopped
- 2 tablespoons unsalted butter, melted
- 1 lemon, thinly sliced
- 2 cloves garlic, minced
- Salt and pepper, to taste
- Parchment paper
- Cooking spray

Instructions:

1. Preheat the Air Fryer: Set your air fryer to 375°F and preheat for about 3 minutes.
2. Prepare the Trout Packets: Cut four pieces of parchment paper large enough to wrap the trout fillets. Place a trout fillet in the center of each piece. Drizzle with melted butter and white wine, sprinkle with chopped dill and minced garlic. Top with lemon slices and season with salt and pepper.
3. Seal the Packets: Fold the parchment paper over the trout fillets to create sealed packets, allowing some space inside for heat circulation.
4. Cook the Trout: Place the packets in the air fryer basket in a single layer. Cook for 12-15 minutes, or until the trout is cooked through and flakes easily with a fork.
5. Serve: Carefully open the packets and serve the trout with the cooking juices and lemon slices.

NUTRITIONAL DATA: CALORIES: 280 | PROTEIN: 25G | CARBOHYDRATES: 3G | FAT: 18G | FIBER: 0G | SUGAR: 0G | SODIUM: 300MG

Lunch and Dinner with Fish

Shrimp Skewers with Garlic and Chili

PREPARATION TIME: 10 MINUTES | COOKING TIME: 8 MINUTES | PORTION SIZE: 4 SERVINGS

Ingredients:

- 1 lb large shrimp, peeled and deveined
- 2 tablespoons olive oil
- 3 cloves garlic, minced
- 1 red chili pepper, finely chopped (or 1/2 teaspoon red pepper flakes)
- 1 tablespoon lemon juice
- 1 tablespoon fresh parsley, chopped
- Salt and pepper, to taste
- Skewers
- Cooking spray

Instructions:

1. Preheat the Air Fryer: Set your air fryer to 400°F (200°C) and preheat for about 3 minutes.
2. Prepare the Shrimp: In a large bowl, toss the shrimp with olive oil, minced garlic, chopped chili pepper (or red pepper flakes), lemon juice, salt, and pepper.
3. Skewer the Shrimp: Thread the shrimp onto skewers, ensuring they are evenly spaced.
4. Cook the Skewers: Lightly spray the air fryer basket with cooking spray. Place the skewers in the basket in a single layer. Cook for 6-8 minutes, flipping halfway through, until the shrimp are pink and cooked through.
5. Serve: Garnish with fresh parsley and serve hot with additional lemon wedges if desired.

NUTRITIONAL DATA: CALORIES: 180 | PROTEIN: 23G | CARBOHYDRATES: 2G | FAT: 8G | FIBER: 0G | SUGAR: 0G | SODIUM: 480MG

Sole in Almond Butter

PREPARATION TIME: 10 MINUTES I COOKING TIME: 10 MINUTES I PORTION SIZE: 4 SERVINGS

Ingredients:

- 4 sole fillets (about 6 oz each)
- 1/4 cup almond flour
- 1/4 cup unsalted butter
- 1/4 cup sliced almonds
- 2 tablespoons lemon juice
- 1 tablespoon fresh parsley, chopped
- Salt and pepper, to taste
- Cooking spray

Instructions:

1. Preheat the Air Fryer: Set your air fryer to 375°F (190°C) and preheat for about 3 minutes.
2. Prepare the Sole: Pat the sole fillets dry with paper towels. Season both sides with salt and pepper, then lightly coat with almond flour.
3. Cook the Sole: Lightly spray the air fryer basket with cooking spray. Place the fillets in the basket in a single layer. Cook for 8-10 minutes, or until the fish is golden brown and cooked through, flipping halfway.
4. Prepare the Almond Butter Sauce: While the fish is cooking, melt the butter in a small skillet over medium heat. Add the sliced almonds and cook until the butter turns golden brown and the almonds are toasted. Stir in the lemon juice and parsley, then remove from heat.
5. Serve: Drizzle the almond butter sauce over the cooked sole fillets and serve immediately.

NUTRITIONAL DATA: CALORIES: 320 | PROTEIN: 25G | CARBOHYDRATES: 4G | FAT: 23G | FIBER: 1G | SUGAR: 1G | SODIUM: 320MG

Halibut Fillet with Basil Pesto

PREPARATION TIME: 10 MINUTES I COOKING TIME: 10 MINUTES I PORTION SIZE: 4 SERVINGS

Ingredients:

- 4 halibut fillets (about 6 oz each)
- 1/4 cup basil pesto (store-bought or homemade)
- 2 tablespoons olive oil
- 1 tablespoon lemon juice
- Salt and pepper, to taste
- Cooking spray
- Fresh basil leaves, for garnish (optional)

Instructions:

1. Preheat the Air Fryer: Set your air fryer to 375°F (190°C) and preheat for about 3 minutes.
2. Prepare the Halibut: Pat the halibut fillets dry with paper towels. Drizzle with olive oil and lemon juice, then season with salt and pepper on both sides.
3. Cook the Halibut: Lightly spray the air fryer basket with cooking spray. Place the halibut fillets in the basket in a single layer. Cook for 8-10 minutes, or until the fish is opaque and flakes easily with a fork.
4. Serve: Top each fillet with a spoonful of basil pesto and garnish with fresh basil leaves if desired. Serve immediately.

NUTRITIONAL DATA: CALORIES: 320 | PROTEIN: 30G | CARBOHYDRATES: 2G | FAT: 22G | FIBER: 0G | SUGAR: 0G | SODIUM: 350MG

Calamari Rings with Aioli Dip

PREPARATION TIME: 15 MINUTES | COOKING TIME: 10 MINUTES | PORTION SIZE: 4 SERVINGS

Ingredients:

- For the Calamari:
- 1 lb calamari rings
- 1/2 cup all-purpose flour
- 1/2 cup breadcrumbs (preferably panko)
- 2 large eggs, beaten
- 1 teaspoon garlic powder
- 1 teaspoon paprika
- Salt and pepper, to taste
- Cooking spray
- For the Aioli Dip:
- 1/2 cup mayonnaise
- 2 cloves garlic, minced
- 1 tablespoon lemon juice
- 1 teaspoon Dijon mustard
- Salt and pepper, to taste

Instructions:

1. Preheat the Air Fryer: Set your air fryer to 400°F (200°C) and preheat for about 3 minutes.
2. Prepare the Calamari Coating: In one bowl, mix the flour with garlic powder, paprika, salt, and pepper. In a second bowl, place the beaten eggs. In a third bowl, add the breadcrumbs.
3. Coat the Calamari Rings: Dredge each calamari ring in the flour mixture, then dip into the beaten eggs, and finally coat with breadcrumbs. Ensure each ring is evenly coated.
4. Cook the Calamari: Lightly spray the air fryer basket with cooking spray. Place the coated calamari rings in the basket in a single layer. Spray the tops lightly with cooking spray as well. Cook for 8-10 minutes, flipping halfway through, until the calamari is golden and crispy.
5. Prepare the Aioli Dip: While the calamari is cooking, mix the mayonnaise, minced garlic, lemon juice, Dijon mustard, salt, and pepper in a small bowl until smooth. Adjust seasoning to taste.
6. Serve: Serve the crispy calamari rings hot with the aioli dip on the side.

NUTRITIONAL DATA: CALORIES: 350 | PROTEIN: 18G | CARBOHYDRATES: 22G | FAT: 20G | FIBER: 1G | SUGAR: 2G | SODIUM: 800MG

Lunch and Dinner with Fish

Flounder Fillets with Tomato Olive Salsa

PREPARATION TIME: 10 MINUTES I COOKING TIME: 10 MINUTES I PORTION SIZE: 4 SERVINGS

Ingredients:

- For the Flounder:
- 4 flounder fillets (about 6 oz each)
- 2 tablespoons olive oil
- Salt and pepper, to taste
- Cooking spray
- For the Tomato Olive Salsa:
- 1 cup cherry tomatoes, halved
- 1/4 cup Kalamata olives, pitted and chopped
- 2 tablespoons red onion, finely chopped
- 2 tablespoons fresh basil, chopped
- 1 tablespoon olive oil
- 1 tablespoon balsamic vinegar
- Salt and pepper, to taste

Instructions:

1. Preheat the Air Fryer: Set your air fryer to 375°F (190°C) and preheat for about 3 minutes.
2. Prepare the Flounder: Pat the flounder fillets dry with paper towels. Drizzle with olive oil and season with salt and pepper on both sides.
3. Cook the Flounder: Lightly spray the air fryer basket with cooking spray. Place the fillets in the basket in a single layer. Cook for 8-10 minutes, or until the fish is opaque and flakes easily with a fork.
4. Prepare the Tomato Olive Salsa: While the fish is cooking, mix the cherry tomatoes, Kalamata olives, red onion, fresh basil, olive oil, balsamic vinegar, salt, and pepper in a bowl.
5. Serve: Top the cooked flounder fillets with the tomato olive salsa and serve immediately.

NUTRITIONAL DATA: CALORIES: 280 | PROTEIN: 25G | CARBOHYDRATES: 5G | FAT: 18G | FIBER: 1G | SUGAR: 2G | SODIUM: 400MG

Lunch and Dinner with Fish

Sea Bream in Paprika Crust

PREPARATION TIME: 10 MINUTES | COOKING TIME: 15 MINUTES | PORTION SIZE: 4 SERVINGS

Ingredients:

- 4 sea bream fillets (about 6 oz each)
- 2 tablespoons olive oil
- 1/4 cup breadcrumbs (preferably panko)
- 1 tablespoon smoked paprika
- 1 teaspoon garlic powder
- 1 teaspoon dried oregano
- Salt and pepper, to taste
- Cooking spray
- Lemon wedges, for serving (optional)

Instructions:

1. Preheat the Air Fryer: Set your air fryer to 375°F (190°C) and preheat for about 3 minutes.
2. Prepare the Paprika Crust: In a small bowl, mix together the breadcrumbs, smoked paprika, garlic powder, dried oregano, salt, and pepper. Drizzle in the olive oil and stir until the mixture is well combined.
3. Coat the Sea Bream: Pat the sea bream fillets dry with paper towels. Press the paprika breadcrumb mixture onto the top of each fillet, ensuring an even coating.
4. Cook the Sea Bream: Lightly spray the air fryer basket with cooking spray. Place the fillets in the basket in a single layer. Cook for 12-15 minutes, or until the crust is golden brown and the fish is cooked through (the fish should flake easily with a fork).
5. Serve: Serve the sea bream fillets hot with lemon wedges on the side if desired.

NUTRITIONAL DATA: CALORIES: 320 | PROTEIN: 28G | CARBOHYDRATES: 8G | FAT: 20G | FIBER: 1G | SUGAR: 1G | SODIUM: 450MG

Sea Bass with Herb Crust

PREPARATION TIME: 10 MINUTES I COOKING TIME: 12 MINUTES I PORTION SIZE: 4 SERVINGS

Ingredients:

- 4 sea bass fillets (about 6 oz each)
- 1/4 cup breadcrumbs (preferably panko)
- 2 tablespoons fresh parsley, chopped
- 1 tablespoon fresh thyme, chopped
- 1 tablespoon fresh rosemary, chopped
- 2 cloves garlic, minced
- Zest of 1 lemon
- 2 tablespoons olive oil
- Salt and pepper, to taste
- Cooking spray
- Lemon wedges, for serving (optional)

Instructions:

1. Preheat the Air Fryer: Set your air fryer to 375°F (190°C) and preheat for about 3 minutes.
2. Prepare the Herb Crust: In a small bowl, combine the breadcrumbs, chopped parsley, thyme, rosemary, minced garlic, lemon zest, salt, and pepper. Drizzle with olive oil and mix until the breadcrumbs are evenly coated.
3. Coat the Sea Bass: Pat the sea bass fillets dry with paper towels. Press the herb breadcrumb mixture onto the top of each fillet, ensuring an even coating.
4. Cook the Sea Bass: Lightly spray the air fryer basket with cooking spray. Place the fillets in the basket in a single layer. Cook for 10-12 minutes, or until the crust is golden brown and the fish is cooked through (it should flake easily with a fork).
5. Serve: Serve the sea bass fillets hot with lemon wedges on the side if desired.

NUTRITIONAL DATA: CALORIES: 300 | PROTEIN: 26G | CARBOHYDRATES: 7G | FAT: 18G | FIBER: 1G | SUGAR: 1G | SODIUM: 400MG

Cod with Sesame Ginger Glaze

PREPARATION TIME: 10 MINUTES | COOKING TIME: 12 MINUTES | PORTION SIZE: 4 SERVINGS

Ingredients:

- 4 cod fillets (about 6 oz each)
- 2 tablespoons soy sauce
- 1 tablespoon sesame oil
- 1 tablespoon honey
- 1 tablespoon fresh ginger, grated
- 2 cloves garlic, minced
- 1 tablespoon rice vinegar
- 1 teaspoon sesame seeds
- 1 tablespoon green onions, chopped (optional)
- Salt and pepper, to taste
- Cooking spray

Instructions:

1. Preheat the Air Fryer: Set your air fryer to 375°F (190°C) and preheat for about 3 minutes.
2. Prepare the Sesame Ginger Glaze: In a small bowl, whisk together the soy sauce, sesame oil, honey, grated ginger, minced garlic, and rice vinegar until well combined.
3. Season the Cod: Pat the cod fillets dry with paper towels. Lightly season both sides with salt and pepper.
4. Coat the Cod with Glaze: Brush the sesame ginger glaze generously over the cod fillets.
5. Cook the Cod: Lightly spray the air fryer basket with cooking spray. Place the fillets in the basket in a single layer. Cook for 10-12 minutes, or until the cod is opaque and flakes easily with a fork.
6. Serve: Garnish with sesame seeds and chopped green onions, if desired. Serve immediately.

NUTRITIONAL DATA: CALORIES: 250 | PROTEIN: 28G | CARBOHYDRATES: 6G | FAT: 12G | FIBER: 1G | SUGAR: 5G | SODIUM: 550MG

Lunch and Dinner with Fish

Salmon Fillet with Herb Crust

PREPARATION TIME: 10 MINUTES | COOKING TIME: 12 MINUTES | PORTION SIZE: 4 SERVINGS

Ingredients:

- 4 salmon fillets (about 6 oz each)
- 1/4 cup breadcrumbs (preferably panko)
- 2 tablespoons fresh parsley, chopped
- 1 tablespoon fresh thyme, chopped
- 1 tablespoon fresh rosemary, chopped
- 2 cloves garlic, minced
- Zest of 1 lemon
- 2 tablespoons olive oil
- Salt and pepper, to taste
- Cooking spray
- Lemon wedges, for serving (optional)

Instructions:

1. Preheat the Air Fryer: Set your air fryer to 375°F (190°C) and preheat for about 3 minutes.
2. Prepare the Herb Crust: In a small bowl, combine the breadcrumbs, chopped parsley, thyme, rosemary, minced garlic, lemon zest, salt, and pepper. Drizzle with olive oil and mix until the breadcrumbs are evenly coated.
3. Coat the Salmon: Pat the salmon fillets dry with paper towels. Press the herb breadcrumb mixture onto the top of each fillet, ensuring an even coating.
4. Cook the Salmon: Lightly spray the air fryer basket with cooking spray. Place the fillets in the basket in a single layer. Cook for 10-12 minutes, or until the crust is golden brown and the salmon is cooked through (it should flake easily with a fork).
5. Serve: Serve the salmon fillets hot with lemon wedges on the side if desired.

NUTRITIONAL DATA: CALORIES: 320 | PROTEIN: 28G | CARBOHYDRATES: 6G | FAT: 20G | FIBER: 1G | SUGAR: 1G | SODIUM: 400MG

Tuna Steaks with Lemon Caper Sauce

PREPARATION TIME: 10 MINUTES | COOKING TIME: 8 MINUTES | PORTION SIZE: 4 SERVINGS

Ingredients:

- 4 tuna steaks (about 6 oz each)
- 2 tablespoons olive oil
- Salt and pepper, to taste
- Cooking spray

For the Lemon Caper Sauce:

- 2 tablespoons unsalted butter
- 2 tablespoons capers, drained
- Juice of 1 lemon
- 2 cloves garlic, minced
- 1 tablespoon fresh parsley, chopped (optional)

Instructions:

1. Preheat the Air Fryer: Set your air fryer to 400°F (200°C) and preheat for about 3 minutes.
2. Season the Tuna: Pat the tuna steaks dry with paper towels. Rub both sides of the steaks with olive oil and season with salt and pepper.
3. Cook the Tuna: Lightly spray the air fryer basket with cooking spray. Place the tuna steaks in the basket in a single layer. Cook for 6-8 minutes, turning halfway through, until the tuna reaches your desired level of doneness (2-3 minutes per side for rare, 4-5 minutes for medium).
4. Prepare the Lemon Caper Sauce: While the tuna is cooking, melt the butter in a small saucepan over medium heat. Add the minced garlic and sauté for 1-2 minutes until fragrant. Stir in the capers and lemon juice, cooking for another 1-2 minutes. Remove from heat and stir in the chopped parsley, if using.
5. Serve: Drizzle the lemon caper sauce over the cooked tuna steaks and serve immediately.

NUTRITIONAL DATA: CALORIES: 320 | PROTEIN: 30G | CARBOHYDRATES: 2G | FAT: 20G | FIBER: 0G | SUGAR: 0G | SODIUM: 450MG

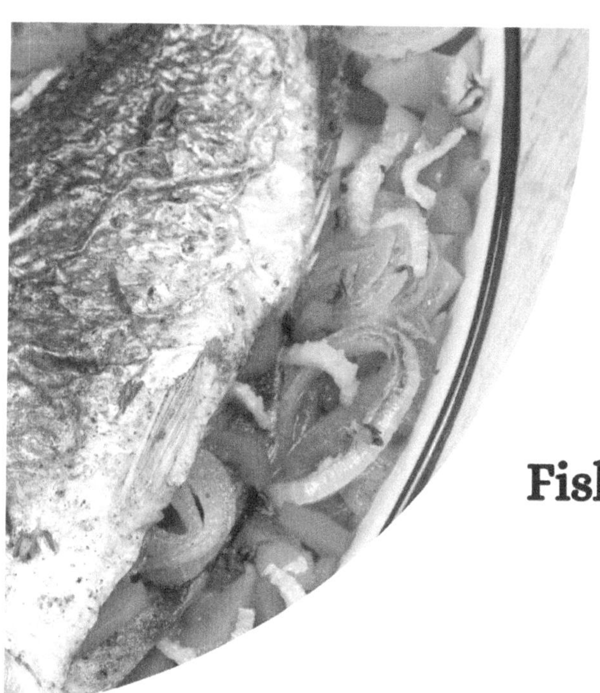

Lunch and Dinner with Fish

Fish with vegetables and peppers

PREPARATION TIME: 10 MINUTES I COOKING TIME: 12 MINUTES I PORTION SIZE: 4 SERVINGS

Ingredients:

- 4 white fish fillets (such as tilapia, cod, or haddock, about 6 oz each)
- 2 tablespoons olive oil
- 1 red bell pepper, sliced
- 1 yellow bell pepper, sliced
- 1 green bell pepper, sliced
- 1 small red onion, sliced
- 2 cloves garlic, minced
- 1 teaspoon paprika
- 1 teaspoon dried oregano
- Salt and pepper, to taste
- Cooking spray
- Lemon wedges, for serving (optional)

Instructions:

1. Preheat the Air Fryer: Set your air fryer to 375°F (190°C) and preheat for about 3 minutes.
2. Prepare the Vegetables: In a large bowl, toss the sliced bell peppers, onion, and minced garlic with 1 tablespoon of olive oil, paprika, oregano, salt, and pepper.
3. Cook the Vegetables: Lightly spray the air fryer basket with cooking spray. Add the seasoned vegetables to the basket and cook for 8 minutes, shaking the basket halfway through.
4. Prepare the Fish: While the vegetables are cooking, pat the fish fillets dry with paper towels. Drizzle the fish with the remaining olive oil and season with salt and pepper on both sides.
5. Cook the Fish: Once the vegetables are cooked, move them to one side of the air fryer basket and place the fish fillets on the other side. Cook for an additional 6-8 minutes, or until the fish is opaque and flakes easily with a fork.
6. Serve: Serve the fish with the cooked peppers and garnish, if desired, with lemon wedges.

NUTRITIONAL DATA: CALORIES: 280 | PROTEIN: 28G | CARBOHYDRATES: 8G | FAT: 14G | FIBER: 3G | SUGAR: 4G | SODIUM: 320MG

Stuffed Eggplants with Quinoa and Pine Nuts

PREPARATION TIME: 15 MINUTES | COOKING TIME: 20 MINUTES | PORTION SIZE: 4 SERVINGS

Ingredients:

- 2 medium eggplants, halved lengthwise
- 1 cup cooked quinoa
- 1/4 cup pine nuts, toasted
- 1/4 cup sun-dried tomatoes, chopped
- 1/4 cup feta cheese, crumbled
- 2 cloves garlic, minced
- 2 tablespoons olive oil
- 1 tablespoon fresh parsley, chopped
- 1 teaspoon dried oregano
- Salt and pepper, to taste
- Cooking spray

Instructions:

1. Preheat the Air Fryer: Set your air fryer to 375°F (190°C) and preheat for about 3 minutes.
2. Prepare the Eggplants: Scoop out the flesh from the eggplant halves, leaving about a 1/2-inch border to create a shell. Lightly brush the eggplant shells with olive oil, season with salt and pepper, and set them aside.
3. Cook the Eggplant Flesh: Chop the scooped-out eggplant flesh into small pieces. In a bowl, toss the chopped eggplant with the minced garlic, oregano, and a little more olive oil. Lightly spray the air fryer basket with cooking spray. Cook the chopped eggplant in the air fryer for 8 minutes, shaking the basket halfway through.
4. Prepare the Quinoa Filling: In a large bowl, combine the cooked quinoa, toasted pine nuts, sun-dried tomatoes, crumbled feta cheese, chopped parsley, and the cooked eggplant mixture. Season with salt and pepper to taste.
5. Stuff the Eggplants: Fill each eggplant shell with the quinoa mixture, pressing it down slightly to pack it in.
6. Cook the Stuffed Eggplants: Place the stuffed eggplants in the air fryer basket in a single layer. Cook for 12-15 minutes, or until the eggplants are tender and the filling is heated through.
7. Serve: Serve the stuffed eggplants hot, garnished with additional parsley if desired.

NUTRITIONAL DATA: CALORIES: 320 | PROTEIN: 8G | CARBOHYDRATES: 28G | FAT: 18G | FIBER: 7G | SUGAR: 6G | SODIUM: 350MG

Vegetarian and Vegan Lunch and Dinner

Sweet Potato Chickpea Burgers

PREPARATION TIME: 15 MINUTES I COOKING TIME: 12 MINUTES I PORTION SIZE: 4 SERVINGS

Ingredients:

- 1 medium sweet potato, peeled and diced
- 1 can (15 oz) chickpeas, drained and rinsed
- 1/4 cup breadcrumbs
- 2 cloves garlic, minced
- 1/4 cup red onion, finely chopped
- 1 tablespoon fresh parsley, chopped
- 1 teaspoon ground cumin
- 1/2 teaspoon smoked paprika
- 1/4 teaspoon cayenne pepper (optional)
- Salt and pepper, to taste
- 1 tablespoon olive oil
- Cooking spray

Instructions:

1. Preheat the Air Fryer: Set your air fryer to 375°F (190°C) and preheat for about 3 minutes.
2. Cook the Sweet Potato: Toss the diced sweet potato with a little olive oil and place in the air fryer basket. Cook for 8-10 minutes until tender. Allow the sweet potato to cool slightly.
3. Prepare the Burger Mixture: In a large bowl, mash the cooked sweet potato and chickpeas together. Add the breadcrumbs, minced garlic, chopped red onion, parsley, cumin, smoked paprika, cayenne pepper (if using), salt, and pepper. Mix until well combined.
4. Form the Patties: Shape the mixture into 4 equal-sized patties. Lightly spray the air fryer basket with cooking spray.
5. Cook the Burgers: Place the patties in the air fryer basket in a single layer. Cook for 10-12 minutes, flipping halfway through, until the burgers are golden brown and firm.
6. Serve: Serve the sweet potato chickpea burgers on buns with your favorite toppings and condiments.

NUTRITIONAL DATA: CALORIES: 240 | PROTEIN: 8G | CARBOHYDRATES: 38G | FAT: 7G | FIBER: 8G | SUGAR: 6G | SODIUM: 350MG

Vegetarian and Vegan Lunch and Dinner

Vegan Lentil Stew with Coconut Milk

PREPARATION TIME: 10 MINUTES | COOKING TIME: 20 MINUTES | PORTION SIZE: 4 SERVINGS

Ingredients:

- 1 cup dried lentils, rinsed
- 1 can (14 oz) coconut milk
- 2 cups vegetable broth
- 1 onion, finely chopped
- 2 cloves garlic, minced
- 1 tablespoon fresh ginger, minced
- 1 teaspoon ground turmeric
- 1 teaspoon ground cumin
- 1/2 teaspoon ground coriander
- 1/4 teaspoon cayenne pepper (optional)
- 1 cup diced tomatoes (fresh or canned)
- 1 carrot, diced
- 1 tablespoon olive oil
- Salt and pepper, to taste
- Fresh cilantro, for garnish (optional)
- Lime wedges, for serving (optional)
- Cooking spray

Instructions:

1. Preheat the Air Fryer: Set your air fryer to 350°F (175°C) and preheat for about 3 minutes.
2. Sauté the Aromatics: Lightly spray an air fryer-safe dish with cooking spray. Add olive oil, onion, garlic, and ginger. Air fry for 5 minutes, stirring halfway, until the onion is soft and translucent.
3. Prepare the Stew: Add the rinsed lentils, turmeric, cumin, coriander, cayenne pepper, diced tomatoes, diced carrot, vegetable broth, and coconut milk to the dish. Stir well to combine all ingredients.
4. Cook the Stew: Air fry at 350°F (175°C) for 15 minutes, stirring halfway through, until the lentils are tender and the stew thickens. If the liquid evaporates too quickly, stir more often or slightly lower the temperature.
5. Serve: Season with salt and pepper to taste. Garnish with fresh cilantro and serve with lime wedges if desired.

NUTRITIONAL DATA: CALORIES: 310 | PROTEIN: 12G | CARBOHYDRATES: 34G | FAT: 15G | FIBER: 8G | SUGAR: 5G | SODIUM: 480MG

Vegetarian and Vegan Lunch and Dinner

Beet Risotto with Walnuts

PREPARATION TIME: 10 MINUTES I COOKING TIME: 18 MINUTES I PORTION SIZE: 4 SERVINGS

Ingredients:

- 1 cup Arborio rice
- 2 medium beets, peeled and grated
- 1 small onion, finely chopped
- 2 cloves garlic, minced
- 4 cups vegetable broth, warmed
- 1/4 cup white wine (optional)
- 1/4 cup walnuts, toasted and chopped
- 2 tablespoons olive oil
- 1/4 cup grated Parmesan cheese (optional for non-vegan)
- Salt and pepper, to taste
- Fresh parsley, for garnish
- Cooking spray

Instructions:

1. Preheat the Air Fryer: Set your air fryer to 350°F (175°C) and preheat for about 3 minutes.
2. Sauté the Aromatics: Lightly spray a small oven-safe dish that fits in your air fryer with cooking spray. Add the olive oil, chopped onion, and minced garlic. Air fry for 5 minutes, stirring halfway through, until the onion is soft and translucent.
3. Cook the Risotto Base: Add the Arborio rice to the dish with the sautéed aromatics, stirring to coat the rice in the oil. Pour in the white wine (if using) and let it simmer for 2 minutes until mostly absorbed.
4. Add the Beets and Broth: Stir in the grated beets. Begin adding the warmed vegetable broth, 1/2 cup at a time, stirring well after each addition. Cover the dish with aluminum foil or a lid that fits.
5. Cook the Risotto: Air fry the covered dish for 10-12 minutes, stirring halfway through, until the rice is creamy and al dente, and the beets are tender.
6. Finish and Serve: Stir in the chopped walnuts and season with salt and pepper to taste. Garnish with fresh parsley and Parmesan cheese if desired.

NUTRITIONAL DATA: CALORIES: 320 | PROTEIN: 8G | CARBOHYDRATES: 50G | FAT: 12G | FIBER: 5G | SUGAR: 7G | SODIUM: 480MG

Vegetarian and Vegan Lunch and Dinner

Zucchini Lasagna

PREPARATION TIME: 15 MINUTES | COOKING TIME: 25 MINUTES | PORTION SIZE: 4 SERVINGS

Ingredients:

- 2 large zucchinis, sliced lengthwise into thin strips
- 1 cup ricotta cheese
- 1/2 cup grated Parmesan cheese
- 1 cup shredded mozzarella cheese
- 1 jar (24 oz) marinara sauce
- 2 garlic cloves, minced
- 1 tablespoon fresh basil, chopped
- 1 tablespoon fresh parsley, chopped
- 1 teaspoon dried oregano
- Salt and pepper, to taste
- Cooking spray

Instructions:

1. Preheat the Air Fryer: Set your air fryer to 375°F (190°C) and preheat for about 3 minutes.
2. Prepare the Zucchini: Lightly salt the zucchini slices and let them sit for 10 minutes to draw out excess moisture. Pat dry with paper towels.
3. Prepare the Cheese Filling: In a bowl, mix the ricotta, grated Parmesan, minced garlic, chopped basil, chopped parsley, dried oregano, salt, and pepper.
4. Assemble the Lasagna: Lightly spray an air fryer-safe baking dish with cooking spray. Begin with a layer of marinara sauce, followed by a layer of zucchini slices, and then a layer of the ricotta mixture. Repeat the layers, finishing with a layer of marinara sauce and topping with shredded mozzarella.
5. Cook the Lasagna: Place the baking dish in the air fryer basket. Cook for 20 minutes. Check, and cook for an additional 5 minutes if needed, until the cheese is melted and bubbly.
6. Serve: Let the lasagna cool for a few minutes before slicing. Serve warm.

NUTRITIONAL DATA: CALORIES: 280 | PROTEIN: 18G | CARBOHYDRATES: 14G | FAT: 18G | FIBER: 3G | SUGARS: 8G | SODIUM: 620MG

Vegetarian and Vegan Lunch and Dinner

Braised Tofu in Ginger Tomato Sauce

PREPARATION TIME: 10 MINUTES I COOKING TIME: 20 MINUTES I PORTION SIZE: 4 SERVINGS

Ingredients:

- 1 block (14 oz) firm tofu, pressed and cut into cubes
- 1 can (14.5 oz) diced tomatoes
- 1 tablespoon tomato paste
- 2 tablespoons soy sauce
- 1 tablespoon fresh ginger, minced
- 3 cloves garlic, minced
- 1 tablespoon olive oil
- 1 teaspoon sugar (optional)
- 1 teaspoon ground cumin
- 1 teaspoon ground coriander
- Salt and pepper, to taste
- Fresh cilantro, for garnish (optional)
- Cooking spray

Instructions:

1. Preheat the Air Fryer: Set your air fryer to 375°F (190°C) and preheat for about 3 minutes.
2. Prepare the Tofu: Lightly spray the air fryer basket with cooking spray. Arrange the tofu cubes in the basket in a single layer. Air fry for 10 minutes, shaking the basket halfway through, until the tofu is golden and slightly crispy.
3. Prepare the Sauce: In a bowl, combine diced tomatoes, tomato paste, soy sauce, minced ginger, minced garlic, cumin, coriander, and sugar (if using). Season with salt and pepper to taste.
4. Combine Tofu and Sauce: Add the crispy tofu to the bowl with the sauce and gently mix to coat the tofu with the sauce.
5. Cook in the Air Fryer: Transfer the tofu and sauce mixture to an air fryer-safe baking dish. Air fry at 375°F (190°C) for 10 minutes, stirring halfway through, until the tofu is well-coated and the sauce thickens slightly.
6. Serve: Garnish with fresh cilantro if desired and serve hot with rice or your preferred side dish.

NUTRITIONAL DATA: CALORIES: 220 | PROTEIN: 12G | CARBOHYDRATES: 14G | FAT: 14G | FIBER: 3G | SUGAR: 5G | SODIUM: 600MG

Mushroom and Spinach Strudel

PREPARATION TIME: 15 MINUTES | COOKING TIME: 20 MINUTES | PORTION SIZE: 4 SERVINGS

Ingredients:

- 1 sheet puff pastry, thawed
- 2 cups fresh spinach, chopped
- 1 cup mushrooms, sliced
- 1 small onion, finely chopped
- 2 cloves garlic, minced
- 1/2 cup ricotta cheese
- 1/4 cup grated Parmesan cheese
- 1 tablespoon olive oil
- 1 teaspoon dried thyme
- Salt and pepper, to taste
- 1 egg, beaten (for egg wash)
- Cooking spray

Instructions:

1. Preheat the Air Fryer: Set your air fryer to 375°F (190°C) and preheat for about 3 minutes.
2. Cook the Filling: Lightly spray a pan with cooking spray and heat the olive oil over medium heat. Add the chopped onion and garlic, and sauté for 2-3 minutes until softened. Add the sliced mushrooms and dried thyme, and cook for another 5 minutes until the mushrooms are browned. Stir in the chopped spinach and cook until wilted. Remove from heat and let it cool slightly.
3. Prepare the Strudel: In a bowl, mix the cooled mushroom-spinach mixture with ricotta cheese, Parmesan cheese, salt, and pepper. Roll out the puff pastry sheet on a lightly floured surface. Spread the filling evenly over the pastry, leaving a small border around the edges. Roll up the pastry tightly, sealing the edges with a little water. Brush the top with beaten egg.
4. Cook the Strudel: Lightly spray the air fryer basket with cooking spray. Place the strudel in the basket seam-side down. Cook for 15-20 minutes, or until the pastry is golden brown and crispy.
5. Serve: Allow the strudel to cool for a few minutes before slicing. Serve warm.

NUTRITIONAL DATA: CALORIES: 350 | PROTEIN: 10G | CARBOHYDRATES: 28G | FAT: 24G | FIBER: 2G | SUGAR: 3G | SODIUM: 450MG

Vegetarian and Vegan Lunch and Dinner

Potato Gnocchi with Tomato Basil Sauce

PREPARATION TIME: 15 MINUTES I COOKING TIME: 25 MINUTES I PORTION SIZE: 4 SERVINGS

Ingredients:

For the Gnocchi:

- 1 lb potato gnocchi (store-bought or homemade)
- 1 tablespoon olive oil
- Salt and pepper, to taste

For the Tomato Basil Sauce:

- 2 cups cherry tomatoes, halved
- 2 cloves garlic, minced
- 1/4 cup fresh basil leaves, chopped
- 1/4 cup tomato sauce
- 1 tablespoon olive oil
- Salt and pepper, to taste
- Grated Parmesan cheese, for serving (optional)
- Cooking spray

Instructions:

1. Prepare the Tomato Basil Sauce in the Air Fryer:
2. Preheat the Air Fryer: Set your air fryer to 350°F (180°C) and preheat for about 3 minutes.
3. Prepare the Sauce: Place the cherry tomatoes, minced garlic, and 1 tablespoon olive oil in an air fryer-safe dish. Season with salt and pepper. Toss to coat. Air fry at 350°F (180°C) for 8-10 minutes until the tomatoes are softened and the sauce begins to form.
4. Add Tomato Sauce and Basil: Stir in the tomato sauce and chopped basil. Air fry for an additional 5 minutes. Adjust seasoning with salt and pepper if needed.
5. Cook the Gnocchi:
6. Prepare the Gnocchi: Toss the potato gnocchi with 1 tablespoon olive oil and season with salt and pepper.
7. Cook the Gnocchi: Lightly spray the air fryer basket with cooking spray. Place the gnocchi in a single layer in the basket. Air fry at 375°F (190°C) for 8-10 minutes, shaking the basket halfway through, until the gnocchi are golden and crispy.
8. Combine and Serve:
9. Mix Gnocchi with Sauce: Toss the crispy gnocchi with the tomato basil sauce until well coated.
10. Serve: Serve immediately, garnished with grated Parmesan cheese if desired.
11. Nutritional Data:

NUTRITIONAL DATA: CALORIES: 320 | PROTEIN: 7G | CARBOHYDRATES: 52G | FAT: 10G | FIBER: 4G | SUGAR: 6G | SODIUM: 480MG

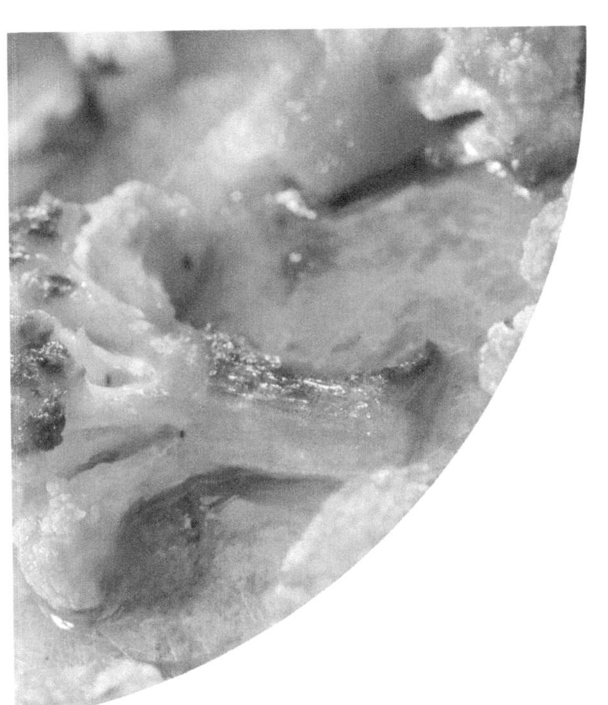

Vegetarian and Vegan Lunch and Dinner

Roasted Cauliflower with Turmeric and Almonds

PREPARATION TIME: 10 MINUTES | COOKING TIME: 15 MINUTES | PORTION SIZE: 4 SERVINGS

Ingredients:

- 1 medium head of cauliflower, cut into florets
- 2 tablespoons olive oil
- 1 teaspoon ground turmeric
- 1/2 teaspoon ground cumin
- 1/4 teaspoon paprika
- 1/4 cup sliced almonds
- Salt and pepper, to taste
- Cooking spray
- Fresh parsley, for garnish (optional)

Instructions:

1. Preheat the Air Fryer: Set your air fryer to 375°F (190°C) and preheat for about 3 minutes.
2. Prepare the Cauliflower: In a large bowl, toss the cauliflower florets with olive oil, ground turmeric, ground cumin, paprika, salt, and pepper until well coated.
3. Cook the Cauliflower: Lightly spray the air fryer basket with cooking spray. Place the seasoned cauliflower in the basket in a single layer. Air fry for 12 minutes, shaking the basket halfway through.
4. Add the Almonds: After 12 minutes, add the sliced almonds to the basket with the cauliflower. Continue to air fry for an additional 3 minutes until the almonds are toasted and the cauliflower is golden and tender.
5. Serve: Garnish with fresh parsley if desired, and serve hot.

NUTRITIONAL DATA: CALORIES: 180 | PROTEIN: 4G | CARBOHYDRATES: 12G | FAT: 14G | FIBER: 5G | SUGAR: 3G | SODIUM: 300MG

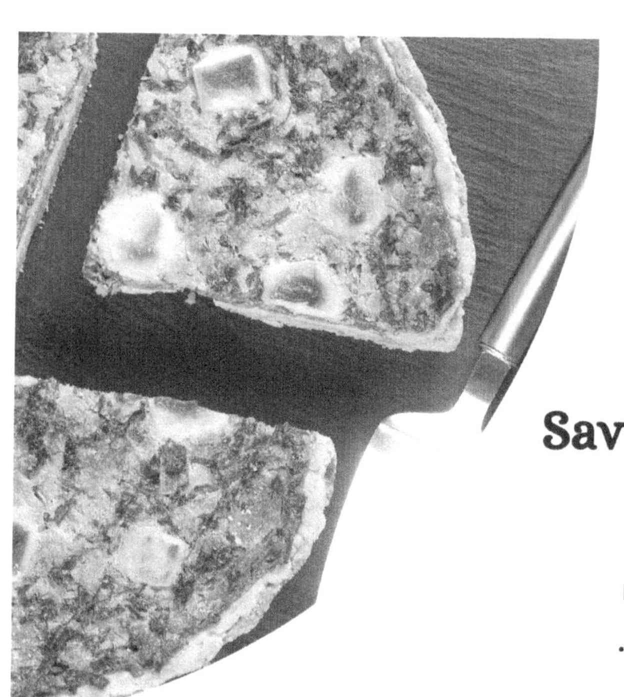

Savory Vegetable and Cheese Tart

PREPARATION TIME: 15 MINUTES I COOKING TIME: 18 MINUTES I PORTION SIZE: 4 SERVINGS

Ingredients:

- 1 roll of puff pastry
- 1 zucchini, thinly sliced
- 1 red bell pepper, sliced
- 1/2 onion, sliced
- 1/2 cup crumbled feta cheese
- 1/2 cup grated cheese (such as Parmesan)
- 2 tablespoons olive oil
- 1/2 teaspoon dried oregano
- Salt and pepper, to taste
- 1 egg, beaten (for brushing)

Instructions:

1. Prepare the Vegetables: Toss the zucchini, bell pepper, and onion slices with olive oil, oregano, salt, and pepper.
2. Prepare the Pastry: Roll out the puff pastry on parchment paper and place it in the air fryer basket.
3. Cook the Vegetables: Cook the vegetables separately in the air fryer or a skillet until tender.
4. Assemble the Tart: Spread the cooked vegetables over the puff pastry, sprinkle with cheeses, and brush the edges with beaten egg.
5. Cook the Tart: Air fry at 350°F (180°C) for 15-18 minutes, until the pastry is golden and crispy.
6. Serve: Let cool slightly before slicing.

NUTRITIONAL DATA: CALORIES: 320 | PROTEIN: 10G | CARBOHYDRATES: 28G | FAT: 20G | FIBER: 3G | SUGAR: 5G | SODIUM: 450MG

Vegetarian and Vegan Lunch and Dinner

Spinach and Feta Savory Pie

PREPARATION TIME: 15 MINUTES | COOKING TIME: 20 MINUTES | PORTION SIZE: 4 SERVINGS

Ingredients:

- 1 roll of puff pastry (store-bought or homemade)
- 2 cups fresh spinach, chopped
- 1/2 cup crumbled feta cheese
- 1/4 cup finely chopped onion
- 2 eggs
- 1/4 cup heavy cream
- 1/4 cup grated Parmesan cheese
- 1 tablespoon olive oil
- Salt and pepper, to taste
- 1 egg, beaten (for brushing)

Instructions:

1. Prepare the Air Fryer: Preheat the air fryer to 375°F (190°C) for about 3 minutes.
2. Cook the Vegetables: Heat olive oil in a non-stick skillet over medium heat. Add the onion and cook until softened, about 3-4 minutes. Add the spinach and cook until wilted. Remove from heat and let cool.
3. Prepare the Filling: In a bowl, combine the cooked spinach and onions with feta cheese, eggs, cream, and Parmesan. Season with salt and pepper.
4. Assemble the Pie: Roll out the puff pastry on a lightly floured surface and trim to fit the air fryer basket. Place the pastry in the basket, pressing the edges to form a crust. Pour the spinach and feta mixture over the pastry.
5. Cook: Brush the pastry edges with the beaten egg. Air fry at 375°F (190°C) for 18-20 minutes, until golden and crispy.
6. Serve: Allow to cool slightly before slicing. Serve warm or at room temperature.

NUTRITIONAL DATA: CALORIES: 320 | PROTEIN: 10G | CARBOHYDRATES: 22G | FAT: 22G | FIBER: 2G | SUGARS: 3G | SODIUM: 450MG

Balsamic-Glazed Carrots with Thyme

PREPARATION TIME: 10 MINUTES | COOKING TIME: 15 MINUTES | PORTION SIZE: 4 SERVINGS

Ingredients:

- 1 lb carrots, peeled and cut into sticks
- 2 tablespoons balsamic vinegar
- 1 tablespoon honey
- 1 tablespoon olive oil
- 1 teaspoon fresh thyme leaves (or 1/2 teaspoon dried thyme)
- Salt and pepper, to taste
- Cooking spray

Instructions:

1. Preheat the Air Fryer: Set your air fryer to 375°F (190°C) and preheat for about 3 minutes.
2. Prepare the Glaze: In a small bowl, whisk together the balsamic vinegar, honey, olive oil, thyme, salt, and pepper.
3. Coat the Carrots: Toss the carrot sticks in the balsamic glaze until they are evenly coated.
4. Cook the Carrots: Lightly spray the air fryer basket with cooking spray. Place the glazed carrots in the basket in a single layer. Air fry for 12-15 minutes, shaking the basket halfway through, until the carrots are tender and slightly caramelized.
5. Serve: Transfer the carrots to a serving dish and garnish with extra thyme if desired.

NUTRITIONAL DATA: CALORIES: 110 | PROTEIN: 1G | CARBOHYDRATES: 17G | FAT: 4G | FIBER: 3G | SUGAR: 12G | SODIUM: 150MG

Kale Chips with Sea Salt and Lemon

PREPARATION TIME: 5 MINUTES | COOKING TIME: 10 MINUTES | PORTION SIZE: 4 SERVINGS

Ingredients:

- 1 bunch kale, stems removed and leaves torn into bite-sized pieces
- 1 tablespoon olive oil
- 1/2 teaspoon sea salt
- Zest of 1 lemon
- 1 tablespoon lemon juice
- Cooking spray

Instructions:

1. Preheat the Air Fryer: Set your air fryer to 350°F (175°C) and preheat for about 3 minutes.
2. Prepare the Kale: In a large bowl, toss the kale pieces with olive oil, lemon juice, sea salt, and lemon zest until evenly coated.
3. Cook the Kale Chips: Lightly spray the air fryer basket with cooking spray. Place the kale in the basket in a single layer, working in batches if necessary. Air fry for 5-7 minutes, shaking the basket halfway through, until the kale is crispy but not burnt.
4. Serve: Let the kale chips cool slightly before serving. Enjoy them as a healthy snack or a side dish.

NUTRITIONAL DATA: CALORIES: 70 | PROTEIN: 2G | CARBOHYDRATES: 7G | FAT: 4G | FIBER: 2G | SUGAR: 1G | SODIUM: 150MG

Vegetarian and Vegan Lunch and Dinner

Pumpkin Quinoa Fritters

PREPARATION TIME: 15 MINUTES I COOKING TIME: 12 MINUTES I PORTION SIZE: 4 SERVINGS

Ingredients:

- 1 cup cooked quinoa
- 1 cup pumpkin puree
- 1/2 cup breadcrumbs (or gluten-free breadcrumbs)
- 1/4 cup grated Parmesan cheese (optional)
- 1/4 cup finely chopped green onions
- 2 cloves garlic, minced
- 1 large egg, beaten
- 1 teaspoon ground cumin
- 1/2 teaspoon ground cinnamon
- Salt and pepper, to taste
- Cooking spray

Instructions:

1. Preheat the Air Fryer: Set your air fryer to 375°F (190°C) and preheat for about 3 minutes.
2. Mix the Fritter Batter: In a large bowl, combine the cooked quinoa, pumpkin puree, breadcrumbs, Parmesan cheese (if using), green onions, garlic, beaten egg, cumin, cinnamon, salt, and pepper. Mix until all ingredients are well incorporated.
3. Form the Fritters: Scoop about 2 tablespoons of the mixture and shape it into small patties or fritters.
4. Cook the Fritters: Lightly spray the air fryer basket with cooking spray. Place the fritters in the basket in a single layer, leaving space between each. Air fry for 10-12 minutes, flipping halfway through, until the fritters are golden brown and crispy.
5. Serve: Serve the fritters warm as an appetizer or side dish. They pair well with a yogurt or tahini dipping sauce.

NUTRITIONAL DATA: CALORIES: 140 | PROTEIN: 5G | CARBOHYDRATES: 22G | FAT: 4G | FIBER: 3G | SUGAR: 3G | SODIUM: 180MG

Eggplant Rolls Stuffed with Vegan Ricotta and Spinach

PREPARATION TIME: 20 MINUTES | COOKING TIME: 15 MINUTES | PORTION SIZE: 4 SERVINGS

Ingredients:

- 2 medium eggplants, sliced lengthwise into 1/4-inch thick slices
- 1 cup vegan ricotta cheese
- 1 cup fresh spinach, chopped
- 2 cloves garlic, minced
- 1 tablespoon olive oil
- 1/4 teaspoon nutmeg
- Salt and pepper, to taste
- 1/2 cup marinara sauce
- Fresh basil leaves, for garnish (optional)
- Cooking spray

Instructions:

1. Preheat the Air Fryer: Set your air fryer to 375°F (190°C) and preheat for about 3 minutes.
2. Prepare the Eggplant: Lightly brush the eggplant slices with olive oil and season with salt and pepper. Place the slices in the air fryer basket in a single layer. Air fry for 8-10 minutes, flipping halfway through, until the eggplant is tender and slightly golden.
3. Prepare the Filling: In a bowl, mix the vegan ricotta, chopped spinach, minced garlic, nutmeg, salt, and pepper until well combined.
4. Assemble the Rolls: Spoon a small amount of the ricotta mixture onto each eggplant slice and roll up tightly. Secure with a toothpick if necessary.
5. Cook the Rolls: Pour a thin layer of marinara sauce into a small baking dish that fits in your air fryer. Place the eggplant rolls on top of the sauce. Lightly spray the tops with cooking spray and air fry for 5-7 minutes, until the rolls are heated through and the sauce is bubbling.
6. Serve: Garnish with fresh basil leaves if desired, and serve hot.

NUTRITIONAL DATA: CALORIES: 150 | PROTEIN: 6G | CARBOHYDRATES: 10G | FAT: 9G | FIBER: 5G | SUGAR: 4G | SODIUM: 320MG

Chapter 5: Snacks and Side Dishes

In this chapter, you'll discover how to make the most of your air fryer to create a variety of delicious and healthy snacks and side dishes. These recipes are designed to be simple and quick, perfect for complementing your main meals or enjoying as tasty bites on their own.

Whether you're looking to prepare crispy appetizers for a gathering, healthy sides for your dinner, or just a quick snack to satisfy your cravings, this section has you covered. From classic favorites like sweet potato fries and kale chips to more inventive dishes like roasted cauliflower with turmeric and almonds, you'll find recipes that are both nutritious and full of flavor.

The air fryer makes it easy to achieve the perfect texture and taste with less oil, ensuring your snacks and side dishes are not only delicious but also healthier. Get ready to enhance your culinary repertoire with these easy-to-follow recipes that are sure to impress your family and friends. Let's dive in and explore the exciting possibilities your air fryer has to offer!

Snacks

Cheese Balls
Vegetable Chips
Sweet Potato Sticks
Crispy Chickpeas
Zucchini Sticks
Celery Fries
Almond-Stuffed Olives
Red Bell Pepper Strips with Goat Cheese Dip
Asian Tofu Cubes with Sesame
Mini Chickpea and Herb Falafel

Side Dishes

Carrot Fries
Cauliflower Florets
Broccoli Nuggets
Spiced Beet Chips
Garlic Herb Potato Wedges
Asian Vegetable Mix with Soy Sauce
Sautéed Mushrooms with Garlic and Parsley
Sweet Potato Gratin with Coconut Milk
Stuffed Mushrooms with Herb Cream Cheese
Crispy Artichoke Hearts with Lemon Dip

Snacks

Cheese Balls

PREPARATION TIME: 10 MINUTES I COOKING TIME: 10 MINUTES I PORTION SIZE: 4 SERVINGS

Ingredients:

- 1 cup shredded cheddar cheese
- 1/2 cup cream cheese, softened
- 1/4 cup grated Parmesan cheese
- 1/4 cup all-purpose flour
- 1 large egg, beaten
- 1/2 teaspoon garlic powder
- 1/2 teaspoon onion powder
- 1/4 teaspoon paprika
- Salt and pepper, to taste
- Cooking spray

Instructions:

1. Preheat the Air Fryer: Set your air fryer to 375°F (190°C) and preheat for about 3 minutes.
2. Prepare the Cheese Balls: In a large bowl, combine the shredded cheddar, cream cheese, Parmesan cheese, flour, garlic powder, onion powder, paprika, salt, and pepper. Mix until well combined.
3. Form the Balls: Roll the cheese mixture into small balls, about 1 inch in diameter. Dip each ball in the beaten egg, then roll in additional flour or breadcrumbs if desired for extra crispiness.
4. Cook the Cheese Balls: Lightly spray the air fryer basket with cooking spray. Place the cheese balls in the basket in a single layer, leaving some space between them. Air fry for 8-10 minutes, shaking the basket halfway through, until the cheese balls are golden brown and crispy.
5. Serve: Serve warm as a snack or appetizer, optionally with a dipping sauce.

NUTRITIONAL DATA: CALORIES: 180 | PROTEIN: 8G | CARBOHYDRATES: 6G | FAT: 14G | FIBER: 0G | SUGAR: 1G | SODIUM: 280MG

Vegetable Chips

PREPARATION TIME: 10 MINUTES I COOKING TIME: 15 MINUTES I PORTION SIZE: 4 SERVINGS

Ingredients:

- 1 large sweet potato, thinly sliced
- 1 large beet, thinly sliced
- 1 zucchini, thinly sliced
- 1 tablespoon olive oil
- 1/2 teaspoon sea salt
- 1/4 teaspoon black pepper
- 1/4 teaspoon smoked paprika (optional)
- Cooking spray

Instructions:

1. Preheat the Air Fryer: Set your air fryer to 350°F (175°C) and preheat for about 3 minutes.
2. Prepare the Vegetables: In a large bowl, toss the thinly sliced vegetables with olive oil, sea salt, black pepper, and smoked paprika (if using) until evenly coated.
3. Cook the Chips: Lightly spray the air fryer basket with cooking spray. Place the vegetable slices in the basket in a single layer, working in batches if necessary. Air fry for 10-15 minutes, shaking the basket halfway through, until the chips are crispy and golden brown.
4. Serve: Let the chips cool slightly before serving. Enjoy them as a healthy snack or side dish.

NUTRITIONAL DATA: CALORIES: 90 | PROTEIN: 2G | CARBOHYDRATES: 15G | FAT: 3G | FIBER: 4G | SUGAR: 5G | SODIUM: 200MG

Sweet Potato Sticks

PREPARATION TIME: 10 MINUTES | COOKING TIME: 15 MINUTES | PORTION SIZE: 4 SERVINGS

Ingredients:

- 2 medium sweet potatoes, peeled and cut into sticks
- 1 tablespoon olive oil
- 1/2 teaspoon sea salt
- 1/4 teaspoon black pepper
- 1/4 teaspoon garlic powder (optional)
- 1/4 teaspoon smoked paprika (optional)
- Cooking spray

Instructions:

1. Preheat the Air Fryer: Set your air fryer to 400°F (200°C) and preheat for about 3 minutes.
2. Prepare the Sweet Potato Sticks: In a large bowl, toss the sweet potato sticks with olive oil, sea salt, black pepper, garlic powder, and smoked paprika (if using) until evenly coated.
3. Cook the Sweet Potato Sticks: Lightly spray the air fryer basket with cooking spray. Place the sweet potato sticks in the basket in a single layer, working in batches if necessary. Air fry for 12-15 minutes, shaking the basket halfway through, until the sticks are crispy on the outside and tender on the inside.
4. Serve: Let the sweet potato sticks cool slightly before serving. Enjoy them as a healthy snack or side dish.

NUTRITIONAL DATA: CALORIES: 120 | PROTEIN: 2G | CARBOHYDRATES: 22G | FAT: 3G | FIBER: 4G | SUGAR: 5G | SODIUM: 180MG

Snacks

Crispy Chickpeas

PREPARATION TIME: 5 MINUTES | COOKING TIME: 15 MINUTES | PORTION SIZE: 4 SERVINGS

Ingredients:

- 1 can (15 oz) chickpeas, drained and rinsed
- 1 tablespoon olive oil
- 1/2 teaspoon sea salt
- 1/2 teaspoon smoked paprika
- 1/4 teaspoon garlic powder
- 1/4 teaspoon ground cumin
- Cooking spray

Instructions:

1. Preheat the Air Fryer: Set your air fryer to 400°F (200°C) and preheat for about 3 minutes.
2. Prepare the Chickpeas: Pat the chickpeas dry with paper towels to remove excess moisture. In a large bowl, toss the chickpeas with olive oil, sea salt, smoked paprika, garlic powder, and ground cumin until evenly coated.
3. Cook the Chickpeas: Lightly spray the air fryer basket with cooking spray. Place the chickpeas in the basket in a single layer. Air fry for 12-15 minutes, shaking the basket every 5 minutes, until the chickpeas are crispy and golden brown.
4. Serve: Let the chickpeas cool slightly before serving. Enjoy them as a healthy snack or salad topping.

NUTRITIONAL DATA: CALORIES: 120 | PROTEIN: 5G | CARBOHYDRATES: 18G | FAT: 4G | FIBER: 6G | SUGAR: 1G | SODIUM: 200MG

Snacks

Zucchini Sticks

PREPARATION TIME: 10 MINUTES I COOKING TIME: 12 MINUTES I PORTION SIZE: 4 SERVINGS

Ingredients:

- 2 medium zucchinis, cut into sticks
- 1/2 cup breadcrumbs (or panko)
- 1/4 cup grated Parmesan cheese
- 1 teaspoon Italian seasoning
- 1/2 teaspoon garlic powder
- 1/2 teaspoon onion powder
- 1/4 teaspoon salt
- 1/4 teaspoon black pepper
- 1 large egg, beaten
- Cooking spray

Instructions:

1. Preheat the Air Fryer: Set your air fryer to 400°F (200°C) and preheat for about 3 minutes.
2. Prepare the Coating: In a shallow bowl, mix together the breadcrumbs, Parmesan cheese, Italian seasoning, garlic powder, onion powder, salt, and pepper.
3. Coat the Zucchini: Dip each zucchini stick into the beaten egg, then roll in the breadcrumb mixture until fully coated.
4. Cook the Zucchini Sticks: Lightly spray the air fryer basket with cooking spray. Place the zucchini sticks in the basket in a single layer. Air fry for 10-12 minutes, shaking the basket halfway through, until the zucchini sticks are golden brown and crispy.
5. Serve: Serve the zucchini sticks warm with your favorite dipping sauce.

NUTRITIONAL DATA: CALORIES: 140 | PROTEIN: 6G | CARBOHYDRATES: 15G | FAT: 6G | FIBER: 2G | SUGAR: 3G | SODIUM: 320MG

Celery Fries

PREPARATION TIME: 10 MINUTES I COOKING TIME: 15 MINUTES I PORTION SIZE: 4 SERVINGS

Ingredients:

- 1 bunch celery, trimmed and cut into fry-sized sticks
- 2 tablespoons olive oil
- 1/2 teaspoon sea salt
- 1/4 teaspoon black pepper
- 1/2 teaspoon garlic powder (optional)
- 1/2 teaspoon paprika (optional)
- Cooking spray

Instructions:

1. Preheat the Air Fryer: Set your air fryer to 375°F (190°C) and preheat for about 3 minutes.
2. Prepare the Celery: In a large bowl, toss the celery sticks with olive oil, sea salt, black pepper, garlic powder, and paprika until evenly coated.
3. Cook the Celery Fries: Lightly spray the air fryer basket with cooking spray. Place the celery sticks in the basket in a single layer, working in batches if necessary. Air fry for 12-15 minutes, shaking the basket halfway through, until the celery fries are crispy and golden brown.
4. Serve: Serve the celery fries warm as a healthy snack or side dish.

NUTRITIONAL DATA: CALORIES: 60 | PROTEIN: 1G | CARBOHYDRATES: 4G | FAT: 4G | FIBER: 2G | SUGAR: 2G | SODIUM: 200MG

Almond-Stuffed Olives

PREPARATION TIME: 5 MINUTES I COOKING TIME: 8 MINUTES I PORTION SIZE: 4 SERVINGS

Ingredients:

- 20 large green olives, pitted
- 20 whole almonds, roasted
- 2 tablespoons all-purpose flour
- 1 large egg, beaten
- 1/4 cup breadcrumbs (or panko)
- 1/4 teaspoon paprika (optional)
- Cooking spray

Instructions:

1. Preheat the Air Fryer: Set your air fryer to 375°F (190°C) and preheat for about 3 minutes.
2. Stuff the Olives: Insert one almond into each pitted olive.
3. Coat the Olives: Roll the stuffed olives in flour, dip them in the beaten egg, and then coat them with breadcrumbs mixed with paprika if desired.
4. Cook the Olives: Lightly spray the air fryer basket with cooking spray. Place the coated olives in the basket in a single layer. Air fry for 6-8 minutes, shaking the basket halfway through, until the olives are golden and crispy.
5. Serve: Serve the almond-stuffed olives warm as an appetizer or snack.

NUTRITIONAL DATA: CALORIES: 100 | PROTEIN: 3G | CARBOHYDRATES: 5G | FAT: 8G | FIBER: 1G | SUGAR: 0G | SODIUM: 250MG

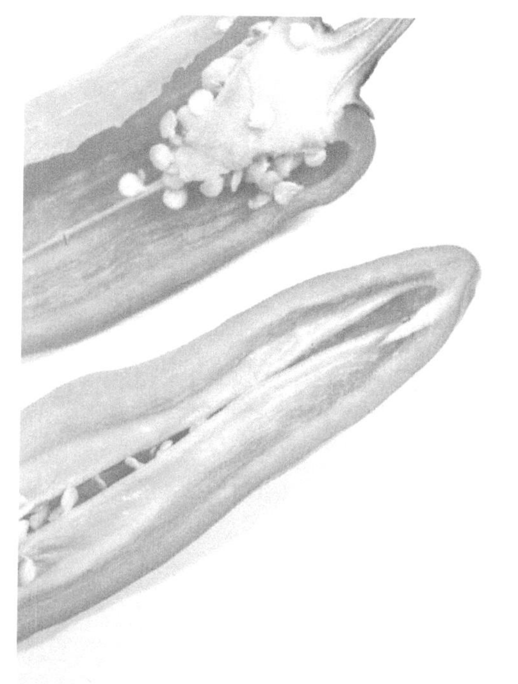

Red Bell Pepper Strips with Goat Cheese Dip

PREPARATION TIME: 10 MINUTES I COOKING TIME: 8 MINUTES I PORTION SIZE: 4 SERVINGS

Ingredients:

- 2 large red bell peppers, cut into strips
- 1 tablespoon olive oil
- 1/2 teaspoon sea salt
- 1/4 teaspoon black pepper
- 4 ounces goat cheese, softened
- 2 tablespoons plain Greek yogurt
- 1 tablespoon fresh chives, chopped
- 1 teaspoon lemon juice
- 1/2 teaspoon garlic powder
- Salt and pepper, to taste
- Cooking spray

Instructions:

1. Preheat the Air Fryer: Set your air fryer to 375°F (190°C) and preheat for about 3 minutes.
2. Prepare the Bell Pepper Strips: Toss the red bell pepper strips with olive oil, sea salt, and black pepper until evenly coated.
3. Cook the Bell Pepper Strips: Lightly spray the air fryer basket with cooking spray. Place the bell pepper strips in the basket in a single layer. Air fry for 6-8 minutes, shaking the basket halfway through, until the peppers are tender and slightly charred.
4. Prepare the Goat Cheese Dip: In a small bowl, mix together the goat cheese, Greek yogurt, chopped chives, lemon juice, garlic powder, salt, and pepper until smooth and creamy.
5. Serve: Serve the warm red bell pepper strips with the goat cheese dip on the side.

NUTRITIONAL DATA: CALORIES: 130 | PROTEIN: 5G | CARBOHYDRATES: 8G | FAT: 9G | FIBER: 2G | SUGAR: 5G | SODIUM: 250MG

Asian Tofu Cubes with Sesame

PREPARATION TIME: 10 MINUTES I COOKING TIME: 15 MINUTES I PORTION SIZE: 4 SERVINGS

Ingredients:

- 1 block (14 oz) firm tofu, pressed and cut into cubes
- 2 tablespoons soy sauce
- 1 tablespoon sesame oil
- 1 tablespoon rice vinegar
- 1 tablespoon honey or maple syrup
- 1 clove garlic, minced
- 1 teaspoon fresh ginger, minced
- 2 tablespoons sesame seeds
- 1 green onion, chopped (optional, for garnish)
- Cooking spray

Instructions:

1. Preheat the Air Fryer: Set your air fryer to 375°F (190°C) and preheat for about 3 minutes.
2. Prepare the Marinade: In a large bowl, mix together the soy sauce, sesame oil, rice vinegar, honey or maple syrup, minced garlic, and minced ginger.
3. Marinate the Tofu: Add the tofu cubes to the marinade and gently toss to coat. Let the tofu marinate for at least 5 minutes to absorb the flavors.
4. Cook the Tofu Cubes: Lightly spray the air fryer basket with cooking spray. Place the marinated tofu cubes in the basket in a single layer. Air fry for 12-15 minutes, shaking the basket halfway through, until the tofu is crispy and golden.
5. Add Sesame Seeds: In the last 2 minutes of cooking, sprinkle the sesame seeds over the tofu cubes in the air fryer, and continue to cook until they are lightly toasted.
6. Serve: Garnish with chopped green onion if desired, and serve the tofu cubes hot as a snack or as a part of a meal.

NUTRITIONAL DATA: CALORIES: 180 | PROTEIN: 10G | CARBOHYDRATES: 7G | FAT: 12G | FIBER: 2G | SUGAR: 3G | SODIUM: 480MG

Snacks

Mini Chickpea and Herb Falafel

PREPARATION TIME: 15 MINUTES I COOKING TIME: 10 MINUTES I PORTION SIZE: 4 SERVINGS

Ingredients:

- 1 can (15 oz) chickpeas, drained and rinsed
- 1/4 cup fresh parsley, chopped
- 1/4 cup fresh cilantro, chopped
- 2 cloves garlic, minced
- 1 small onion, chopped
- 1 teaspoon ground cumin
- 1 teaspoon ground coriander
- 1/4 teaspoon ground cayenne pepper (optional)
- 1 teaspoon baking powder
- 2 tablespoons all-purpose flour (or chickpea flour for a gluten-free option)
- Salt and pepper, to taste
- 2 tablespoons olive oil
- Cooking spray

Instructions:

1. Preheat the Air Fryer: Set your air fryer to 375°F (190°C) and preheat for about 3 minutes.
2. Prepare the Falafel Mixture: In a food processor, combine the chickpeas, parsley, cilantro, garlic, onion, cumin, coriander, cayenne pepper (if using), baking powder, flour, salt, and pepper. Pulse until the mixture is well combined but still slightly chunky.
3. Form the Falafel: Shape the mixture into small balls, about 1 inch in diameter. Lightly flatten each ball to create mini falafel patties.
4. Cook the Falafel: Lightly spray the air fryer basket with cooking spray. Arrange the falafel in the basket in a single layer. Lightly brush or spray the tops of the falafel with olive oil. Air fry for 8-10 minutes, flipping halfway through, until the falafel are golden brown and crispy.
5. Serve: Serve the mini falafel warm with your favorite dipping sauce or as part of a pita or salad.

NUTRITIONAL DATA: CALORIES: 150 | PROTEIN: 6G | CARBOHYDRATES: 18G | FAT: 6G | FIBER: 5G | SUGAR: 2G | SODIUM: 300MG

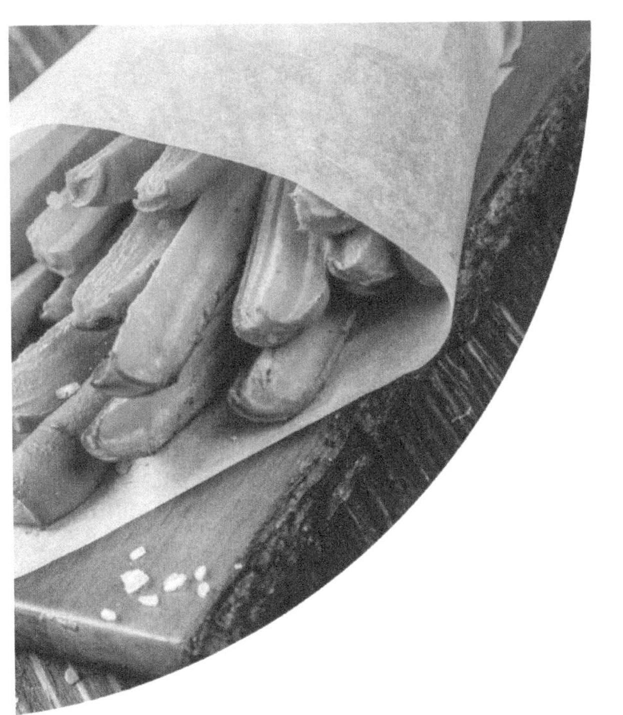

Carrot Fries

PREPARATION TIME: 10 MINUTES | COOKING TIME: 15 MINUTES | PORTION SIZE: 4 SERVINGS

Ingredients:

- 4 large carrots, peeled and cut into fry-sized sticks
- 1 tablespoon olive oil
- 1/2 teaspoon sea salt
- 1/4 teaspoon black pepper
- 1/2 teaspoon garlic powder (optional)
- 1/2 teaspoon smoked paprika (optional)
- Cooking spray

Instructions:

1. Preheat the Air Fryer: Set your air fryer to 375°F (190°C) and preheat for about 3 minutes.
2. Prepare the Carrot Fries: In a large bowl, toss the carrot sticks with olive oil, sea salt, black pepper, garlic powder, and smoked paprika until evenly coated.
3. Cook the Carrot Fries: Lightly spray the air fryer basket with cooking spray. Place the carrot sticks in the basket in a single layer, working in batches if necessary. Air fry for 12-15 minutes, shaking the basket halfway through, until the carrot fries are tender and slightly crispy.
4. Serve: Serve the carrot fries warm as a healthy snack or side dish.

NUTRITIONAL DATA: CALORIES: 80 | PROTEIN: 1G | CARBOHYDRATES: 12G | FAT: 3G | FIBER: 3G | SUGAR: 5G | SODIUM: 200MG

Side Dishes

Cauliflower Florets

PREPARATION TIME: 5 MINUTES I COOKING TIME: 12 MINUTES I PORTION SIZE: 4 SERVINGS

Ingredients:

- 1 medium cauliflower, cut into florets
- 2 tablespoons olive oil
- 1/2 teaspoon sea salt
- 1/4 teaspoon black pepper
- 1/2 teaspoon garlic powder (optional)
- 1/2 teaspoon smoked paprika (optional)
- Cooking spray

Instructions:

1. Preheat the Air Fryer: Set your air fryer to 400°F (200°C) and preheat for about 3 minutes.
2. Prepare the Cauliflower: In a large bowl, toss the cauliflower florets with olive oil, sea salt, black pepper, garlic powder, and smoked paprika until evenly coated.
3. Cook the Cauliflower: Lightly spray the air fryer basket with cooking spray. Place the cauliflower florets in the basket in a single layer, working in batches if necessary. Air fry for 10-12 minutes, shaking the basket halfway through, until the cauliflower is golden and tender.
4. Serve: Serve the cauliflower florets warm as a healthy snack or side dish.

NUTRITIONAL DATA: CALORIES: 90 | PROTEIN: 3G | CARBOHYDRATES: 7G | FAT: 5G | FIBER: 3G | SUGAR: 2G | SODIUM: 220MG

Broccoli Nuggets

PREPARATION TIME: 10 MINUTES I COOKING TIME: 12 MINUTES I PORTION SIZE: 4 SERVINGS

Ingredients:

- 2 cups broccoli florets, finely chopped
- 1/2 cup breadcrumbs (or panko)
- 1/2 cup shredded cheddar cheese
- 1/4 cup grated Parmesan cheese
- 1 large egg, beaten
- 1 clove garlic, minced
- 1/4 teaspoon onion powder
- 1/4 teaspoon black pepper
- 1/4 teaspoon salt
- Cooking spray

Instructions:

1. Preheat the Air Fryer: Set your air fryer to 375°F (190°C) and preheat for about 3 minutes.
2. Prepare the Mixture: In a large bowl, combine the chopped broccoli, breadcrumbs, cheddar cheese, Parmesan cheese, beaten egg, minced garlic, onion powder, black pepper, and salt. Mix until well combined.
3. Form the Nuggets: Shape the mixture into small nugget-sized patties.
4. Cook the Nuggets: Lightly spray the air fryer basket with cooking spray. Place the nuggets in the basket in a single layer. Air fry for 10-12 minutes, flipping halfway through, until the nuggets are golden brown and crispy.
5. Serve: Serve the broccoli nuggets warm with your favorite dipping sauce.

NUTRITIONAL DATA: CALORIES: 110 | PROTEIN: 6G | CARBOHYDRATES: 10G | FAT: 6G | FIBER: 2G | SUGAR: 1G | SODIUM: 250MG

Side Dishes

Spiced Beet Chips

PREPARATION TIME: 10 MINUTES I COOKING TIME: 15 MINUTES I PORTION SIZE: 4 SERVINGS

Ingredients:

- 3 medium beets, peeled and thinly sliced
- 1 tablespoon olive oil
- 1/2 teaspoon sea salt
- 1/4 teaspoon black pepper
- 1/4 teaspoon smoked paprika
- 1/4 teaspoon ground cumin
- Cooking spray

Instructions:

1. Preheat the Air Fryer: Set your air fryer to 350°F (175°C) and preheat for about 3 minutes.
2. Prepare the Beets: In a large bowl, toss the beet slices with olive oil, sea salt, black pepper, smoked paprika, and ground cumin until evenly coated.
3. Cook the Beet Chips: Lightly spray the air fryer basket with cooking spray. Place the beet slices in the basket in a single layer, working in batches if necessary. Air fry for 12-15 minutes, shaking the basket halfway through, until the beet chips are crispy.
4. Serve: Let the beet chips cool slightly before serving. Enjoy them as a healthy snack.

NUTRITIONAL DATA: CALORIES: 80 | PROTEIN: 2G | CARBOHYDRATES: 15G | FAT: 3G | FIBER: 4G | SUGAR: 8G | SODIUM: 210MG

Side Dishes

Garlic Herb Potato Wedges

PREPARATION TIME: 10 MINUTES I COOKING TIME: 20 MINUTES I PORTION SIZE: 4 SERVINGS

Ingredients:

- 4 medium russet potatoes, cut into wedges
- 2 tablespoons olive oil
- 2 cloves garlic, minced
- 1 teaspoon dried rosemary
- 1 teaspoon dried thyme
- 1/2 teaspoon sea salt
- 1/4 teaspoon black pepper
- 1/4 teaspoon smoked paprika (optional)
- Cooking spray

Instructions:

1. Preheat the Air Fryer: Set your air fryer to 400°F (200°C) and preheat for about 3 minutes.
2. Prepare the Potato Wedges: In a large bowl, toss the potato wedges with olive oil, minced garlic, rosemary, thyme, sea salt, black pepper, and smoked paprika (if using) until evenly coated.
3. Cook the Potato Wedges: Lightly spray the air fryer basket with cooking spray. Place the potato wedges in the basket in a single layer, working in batches if necessary. Air fry for 18-20 minutes, shaking the basket halfway through, until the wedges are crispy and golden brown.
4. Serve: Serve the garlic herb potato wedges hot as a side dish or snack.

NUTRITIONAL DATA: CALORIES: 180 | PROTEIN: 3G | CARBOHYDRATES: 30G | FAT: 6G | FIBER: 3G | SUGAR: 2G | SODIUM: 320MG

Side Dishes

Asian Vegetable Mix with Soy Sauce

PREPARATION TIME: 10 MINUTES I COOKING TIME: 12 MINUTES I PORTION SIZE: 4 SERVINGS

Ingredients:

- 1 cup broccoli florets
- 1 cup sliced bell peppers (red, yellow, or green)
- 1 cup snap peas
- 1 cup sliced carrots
- 1 tablespoon soy sauce
- 1 tablespoon sesame oil
- 1 teaspoon minced garlic
- 1 teaspoon minced ginger
- 1/2 teaspoon red pepper flakes (optional)
- Cooking spray

Instructions:

1. Preheat the Air Fryer: Set your air fryer to 375°F (190°C) and preheat for about 3 minutes.
2. Prepare the Vegetables: In a large bowl, toss the broccoli, bell peppers, snap peas, and carrots with soy sauce, sesame oil, minced garlic, minced ginger, and red pepper flakes if using, until evenly coated.
3. Cook the Vegetable Mix: Lightly spray the air fryer basket with cooking spray. Place the vegetable mix in the basket in a single layer. Air fry for 10-12 minutes, shaking the basket halfway through, until the vegetables are tender and slightly charred.
4. Serve: Serve the Asian vegetable mix warm as a side dish or over rice for a light meal.

NUTRITIONAL DATA: CALORIES: 90 | PROTEIN: 3G | CARBOHYDRATES: 12G | FAT: 4G | FIBER: 4G | SUGAR: 5G | SODIUM: 320MG

Sautéed Mushrooms with Garlic and Parsley

PREPARATION TIME: 5 MINUTES | COOKING TIME: 10 MINUTES | PORTION SIZE: 4 SERVINGS

Ingredients:

- 2 cups mushrooms, sliced
- 2 tablespoons olive oil
- 3 cloves garlic, minced
- 1/4 cup fresh parsley, chopped
- 1/2 teaspoon sea salt
- 1/4 teaspoon black pepper
- Cooking spray

Instructions:

1. Preheat the Air Fryer: Set your air fryer to 375°F (190°C) and preheat for about 3 minutes.
2. Prepare the Mushrooms: Toss the mushrooms in olive oil, minced garlic, sea salt, and black pepper.
3. Cook the Mushrooms: Air fry the mushrooms, shaking the basket halfway through until tender and golden.
4. Serve: Garnish with fresh parsley.

NUTRITIONAL DATA: CALORIES: 90 | PROTEIN: 2G | CARBOHYDRATES: 5G | FAT: 7G | FIBER: 1G | SODIUM: 200MG

Side Dishes

Sweet Potato Gratin with Coconut Milk

PREPARATION TIME: 15 MINUTES I COOKING TIME: 25 MINUTES I PORTION SIZE: 4 SERVINGS

Ingredients:

- 2 large sweet potatoes, peeled and thinly sliced
- 1 can (14 oz) coconut milk
- 1/4 cup grated Parmesan cheese (optional for a non-vegan option)
- 2 cloves garlic, minced
- 1/2 teaspoon sea salt
- 1/4 teaspoon black pepper
- 1/4 teaspoon ground nutmeg
- 1 tablespoon olive oil
- Fresh thyme, for garnish (optional)
- Cooking spray

Instructions:

1. Preheat the Air Fryer: Set your air fryer to 375°F (190°C) and preheat for about 3 minutes.
2. Prepare the Gratin: In a mixing bowl, combine the coconut milk, minced garlic, sea salt, black pepper, and ground nutmeg. Toss the sweet potato slices in this mixture until they are well coated.
3. Layer the Sweet Potatoes: Lightly spray an air fryer-safe baking dish with cooking spray. Layer the sweet potato slices in the dish, pouring the coconut milk mixture over each layer. If using Parmesan cheese, sprinkle it between the layers.
4. Cook the Gratin: Place the baking dish in the air fryer basket. Air fry for 20-25 minutes, or until the sweet potatoes are tender and the top is golden brown.
5. Serve: Garnish with fresh thyme if desired. Serve the gratin warm as a side dish.

NUTRITIONAL DATA: CALORIES: 250 | PROTEIN: 3G | CARBOHYDRATES: 32G | FAT: 12G | FIBER: 4G | SUGAR: 7G | SODIUM: 350MG

Side Dishes

Stuffed Mushrooms with Herb Cream Cheese

PREPARATION TIME: 10 MINUTES I COOKING TIME: 10 MINUTES I PORTION SIZE: 4 SERVINGS

Ingredients:

- 12 large button mushrooms, stems removed
- 4 oz (115g) cream cheese, softened
- 2 tablespoons fresh parsley, chopped
- 1 tablespoon fresh chives, chopped
- 1 garlic clove, minced
- 1/4 teaspoon sea salt
- 1/4 teaspoon black pepper
- 1/4 cup breadcrumbs (optional for added crunch)
- 1 tablespoon grated Parmesan cheese (optional)
- Cooking spray

Instructions:

1. Preheat the Air Fryer: Set your air fryer to 375°F (190°C) and preheat for about 3 minutes.
2. Prepare the Filling: In a bowl, combine the softened cream cheese, parsley, chives, garlic, sea salt, and black pepper until well mixed.
3. Stuff the Mushrooms: Fill each mushroom cap with the herb cream cheese mixture. If desired, sprinkle breadcrumbs and Parmesan cheese on top of the stuffed mushrooms.
4. Cook the Mushrooms: Lightly spray the air fryer basket with cooking spray. Place the stuffed mushrooms in the basket in a single layer. Air fry for 8-10 minutes, until the mushrooms are tender and the tops are golden.
5. Serve: Serve the stuffed mushrooms warm as an appetizer or side dish.

NUTRITIONAL DATA: CALORIES: 120 | PROTEIN: 4G | CARBOHYDRATES: 6G | FAT: 9G | FIBER: 1G | SUGAR: 2G | SODIUM: 250MG

Side Dishes

Crispy Artichoke Hearts with Lemon Dip

PREPARATION TIME: 10 MINUTES I COOKING TIME: 12 MINUTES I PORTION SIZE: 4 SERVINGS

Ingredients:

- 1 can (14 oz) artichoke hearts, drained and halved
- 1/2 cup breadcrumbs (or panko)
- 1/4 cup grated Parmesan cheese
- 1 teaspoon garlic powder
- 1/2 teaspoon sea salt
- 1/4 teaspoon black pepper
- 2 tablespoons olive oil
- Cooking spray

For the Lemon Dip:

- 1/2 cup plain Greek yogurt
- 1 tablespoon fresh lemon juice
- 1 teaspoon lemon zest
- 1 teaspoon fresh dill, chopped
- Salt and pepper, to taste

Instructions:

1. Preheat the Air Fryer: Set your air fryer to 375°F (190°C) and preheat for about 3 minutes.
2. Prepare the Artichoke Hearts: In a bowl, toss the artichoke hearts with olive oil, ensuring they are evenly coated.
3. Coat the Artichokes: In another bowl, mix together the breadcrumbs, Parmesan cheese, garlic powder, sea salt, and black pepper. Dredge the artichoke hearts in the breadcrumb mixture, pressing lightly to adhere.
4. Cook the Artichoke Hearts: Lightly spray the air fryer basket with cooking spray. Place the coated artichoke hearts in the basket in a single layer. Air fry for 10-12 minutes, shaking the basket halfway through, until they are crispy and golden.
5. Prepare the Lemon Dip: While the artichokes are cooking, mix together the Greek yogurt, lemon juice, lemon zest, dill, salt, and pepper in a small bowl.
6. Serve: Serve the crispy artichoke hearts warm with the lemon dip on the side.

NUTRITIONAL DATA: CALORIES: 180 | PROTEIN: 6G | CARBOHYDRATES: 16G | FAT: 10G | FIBER: 5G | SUGAR: 2G | SODIUM: 450MG

Chapter 6: Desserts

Here, you'll explore a variety of delicious and healthier dessert options that you can easily prepare using your air fryer. These recipes are crafted to satisfy your sweet tooth while utilizing the unique benefits of air frying.

The air fryer allows you to create desserts with perfect textures, whether you prefer crispy, gooey, or fluffy treats, all with less oil and reduced cooking time compared to traditional methods. From classic favorites to innovative new creations, this section provides a range of recipes that are both simple to make and delightful to eat.

Discover how your air fryer can help you whip up mouth-watering desserts with ease, making every meal end on a sweet note without the guilt. Whether you're a beginner or a seasoned cook, these dessert recipes are designed to be accessible and rewarding, ensuring that you can enjoy your favorite sweets in a healthier way.

Let's embark on this sweet culinary journey and uncover the endless possibilities your air fryer has to offer for creating delightful desserts!

Mini Apple Strudels
Pear Tartelettes
Almond Vanilla Crescents
Pistachio Cheesecakes
Lemon Lime Bars
Strawberry Ricotta Fritters
Hazelnut Brownie Cubes
Blueberry Crumble Muffins
Air Fryer Cinnamon Sugar Donuts
Lemon Ricotta Tarts
Pear Cinnamon Tart
Chocolate biscuits
Apple Pies from Hot Air Fryer
Banana Cake with Chocolate Chips
Raspberry Tarts

Desserts

Mini Apple Strudels

PREPARATION TIME: 15 MINUTES I COOKING TIME: 12 MINUTES I PORTION SIZE: 4 SERVINGS

Ingredients:

- 1 sheet of puff pastry, thawed and cut into 8 rectangles
- 2 medium apples, peeled, cored, and finely chopped
- 1/4 cup granulated sugar
- 1 teaspoon ground cinnamon
- 1/4 teaspoon ground nutmeg
- 1 tablespoon lemon juice
- 1/4 cup raisins (optional)
- 1 tablespoon all-purpose flour
- 1 egg, beaten (for egg wash)
- Powdered sugar (for dusting)
- Cooking spray

Instructions:

1. Preheat the Air Fryer: Set your air fryer to 350°F (175°C) and preheat for about 3 minutes.
2. Prepare the Filling: In a medium bowl, combine the chopped apples, sugar, cinnamon, nutmeg, lemon juice, raisins (if using), and flour. Mix until the apples are well coated.
3. Assemble the Strudels: Place a spoonful of the apple mixture onto one half of each puff pastry rectangle, leaving space around the edges. Fold the other half over the filling, sealing the edges with a fork. Brush the tops with the beaten egg.
4. Cook the Strudels: Lightly spray the air fryer basket with cooking spray. Place the strudels in the basket in a single layer, working in batches if necessary. Air fry for 10-12 minutes, until the strudels are golden and puffy.
5. Serve: Dust with powdered sugar before serving warm.

NUTRITIONAL DATA: CALORIES: 240 | PROTEIN: 3G | CARBOHYDRATES: 32G | FAT: 12G | FIBER: 2G | SUGAR: 14G | SODIUM: 150MG

Pear Tartelettes

PREPARATION TIME: 15 MINUTES I COOKING TIME: 15 MINUTES I PORTION SIZE: 4 SERVINGS

Ingredients:

- 1 sheet of puff pastry, thawed and cut into 4 squares
- 2 ripe pears, peeled, cored, and thinly sliced
- 2 tablespoons honey
- 1/2 teaspoon ground cinnamon
- 1/4 teaspoon ground nutmeg
- 1/4 cup almond flour
- 1 tablespoon butter, melted
- 1 egg, beaten (for egg wash)
- Powdered sugar (for dusting, optional)
- Cooking spray

Instructions:

1. Preheat the Air Fryer: Set your air fryer to 350°F (175°C) and preheat for about 3 minutes.
2. Prepare the Pears: In a bowl, toss the pear slices with honey, cinnamon, and nutmeg until evenly coated.
3. Assemble the Tartelettes: Place a small amount of almond flour in the center of each puff pastry square. Arrange the pear slices on top of the almond flour in a fanned-out pattern. Drizzle with melted butter. Fold the edges of the puff pastry over the pears to create a border. Brush the edges with the beaten egg.
4. Cook the Tartelettes: Lightly spray the air fryer basket with cooking spray. Place the tartelettes in the basket in a single layer, working in batches if necessary. Air fry for 12-15 minutes, until the pastry is golden and the pears are tender.
5. Serve: Dust with powdered sugar if desired and serve warm.

NUTRITIONAL DATA: CALORIES: 290 | PROTEIN: 4G | CARBOHYDRATES: 36G | FAT: 15G | FIBER: 4G | SUGAR: 14G | SODIUM: 200MG

Desserts

Almond Vanilla Crescents

PREPARATION TIME: 20 MINUTES I COOKING TIME: 12 MINUTES I PORTION SIZE: 12 SERVINGS

Ingredients:

- 1 cup almond flour
- 1/2 cup all-purpose flour
- 1/4 cup powdered sugar
- 1/2 cup unsalted butter, softened
- 1/4 cup granulated sugar
- 1 teaspoon vanilla extract
- 1/2 teaspoon almond extract
- 1/4 cup sliced almonds
- Powdered sugar, for dusting

Instructions:

1. Preheat the Air Fryer: Set your air fryer to 325°F (160°C) and preheat for about 3 minutes.
2. Prepare the Dough: In a mixing bowl, cream together the butter, powdered sugar, and granulated sugar until light and fluffy. Add the vanilla and almond extracts and mix well. Gradually add the almond flour and all-purpose flour, mixing until a soft dough forms. Stir in the sliced almonds.
3. Shape the Crescents: Divide the dough into 12 equal portions. Roll each portion into a small log and then shape it into a crescent.
4. Cook the Crescents: Place the crescents in the air fryer basket, leaving space between each one. Air fry for 10-12 minutes, or until the crescents are lightly golden.
5. Serve: Let the crescents cool slightly, then dust with powdered sugar before serving.

NUTRITIONAL DATA: CALORIES: 140 | PROTEIN: 3G | CARBOHYDRATES: 10G | FAT: 10G | FIBER: 1G | SUGAR: 5G | SODIUM: 40MG

Pistachio Cheesecakes

PREPARATION TIME: 20 MINUTES I COOKING TIME: 15 MINUTES I PORTION SIZE: 6 MINI CHEESECAKES

Ingredients:

- 1 cup graham cracker crumbs
- 1/4 cup melted butter
- 1/2 cup shelled pistachios, finely chopped
- 8 oz cream cheese, softened
- 1/4 cup granulated sugar
- 1 large egg
- 1/4 cup sour cream
- 1 teaspoon vanilla extract
- 1/4 teaspoon almond extract
- Additional chopped pistachios for garnish

Instructions:

1. Preheat the Air Fryer: Set your air fryer to 320°F (160°C) and preheat for about 3 minutes.
2. Prepare the Crust: In a bowl, combine the graham cracker crumbs, melted butter, and chopped pistachios. Press the mixture into the bottom of an air fryer-safe silicone mold, filling each compartment about 1/4 inch thick.
3. Prepare the Cheesecake Filling: In a separate bowl, beat the cream cheese and sugar until smooth. Add the egg, sour cream, vanilla extract, and almond extract, and mix until fully combined.
4. Assemble the Cheesecakes: Pour the cheesecake filling over the prepared crust in each mold compartment, filling almost to the top.
5. Cook the Cheesecakes: Place the silicone mold in the air fryer basket and cook at 320°F (160°C) for 12-15 minutes, or until the cheesecakes are set and slightly puffed. They will firm up as they cool.
6. Cool and Serve: Allow the cheesecakes to cool completely in the mold. Once cooled, remove them from the mold and garnish with additional chopped pistachios before serving.

NUTRITIONAL DATA: CALORIES: 250 | PROTEIN: 4G | CARBOHYDRATES: 20G | FAT: 18G | FIBER: 1G | SUGAR: 12G | SODIUM: 180MG

Lemon Lime Bars

PREPARATION TIME: 15 MINUTES I COOKING TIME: 20 MINUTES I PORTION SIZE: 8 SERVINGS

Ingredients:

- 1 cup all-purpose flour
- 1/4 cup powdered sugar
- 1/2 cup unsalted butter, melted
- 3/4 cup granulated sugar
- 2 large eggs
- 1/4 cup lemon juice
- 1/4 cup lime juice
- 1 tablespoon lemon zest
- 1 tablespoon lime zest
- 1/2 teaspoon baking powder
- Powdered sugar, for dusting

Instructions:

1. Preheat the Air Fryer: Set your air fryer to 350°F (175°C) and preheat for about 3 minutes.
2. Prepare the Crust: In a medium bowl, combine the flour, powdered sugar, and melted butter. Mix until the dough comes together. Press the dough evenly into the bottom of an air fryer-safe mold.
3. Cook the Crust: Place the mold in the air fryer and cook the crust for 10 minutes, or until lightly golden.
4. Prepare the Filling: While the crust is baking, whisk together the granulated sugar, eggs, lemon juice, lime juice, lemon zest, lime zest, and baking powder until smooth.
5. Add the Filling: Pour the lemon-lime mixture over the pre-baked crust in the mold.
6. Cook the Bars: Return the mold to the air fryer and cook for an additional 10 minutes, or until the filling is set and the top is lightly browned.
7. Cool and Serve: Allow the bars to cool completely before cutting them into squares. Dust with powdered sugar before serving.

NUTRITIONAL DATA: CALORIES: 180 | PROTEIN: 2G | CARBOHYDRATES: 25G | FAT: 8G | FIBER: 1G | SUGAR: 18G | SODIUM: 70MG

Strawberry Ricotta Fritters

PREPARATION TIME: 15 MINUTES I COOKING TIME: 10 MINUTES I PORTION SIZE: 4 SERVINGS

Ingredients:

- 1 cup ricotta cheese
- 1/2 cup all-purpose flour
- 2 tablespoons granulated sugar
- 1 teaspoon vanilla extract
- 1 large egg
- 1 teaspoon baking powder
- 1/4 teaspoon salt
- 1/2 cup fresh strawberries, diced
- Powdered sugar, for dusting
- Cooking spray

Instructions:

1. In einer großen Schüssel Ricotta, Mehl, Zucker, Ei und Vanilleextrakt zu einem glatten Teig verrühren.
2. Die gewürfelten Erdbeeren vorsichtig unterheben.
3. Kleine Löffelportionen des Teiges in Silikonformen geben, die für die Heißluftfritteuse geeignet sind.
4. Die Fritters bei 180°C (356°F) in der Heißluftfritteuse für etwa 8 Minuten backen, bis sie goldbraun und fest sind.
5. Die fertigen Fritters aus der Fritteuse nehmen und vor dem Servieren mit Puderzucker bestäuben.

NUTRITIONAL DATA: CALORIES: 180 | PROTEIN: 6G | CARBOHYDRATES: 18G | FAT: 9G | FIBER: 1G | SUGAR: 7G | SODIUM: 180MG

Desserts

Hazelnut Brownie Cubes

PREPARATION TIME: 15 MINUTES I COOKING TIME: 15 MINUTES I PORTION SIZE: 9 SERVINGS

Ingredients:

- 1/2 cup unsalted butter, melted
- 1/2 cup granulated sugar
- 1/4 cup brown sugar
- 2 large eggs
- 1 teaspoon vanilla extract
- 1/3 cup all-purpose flour
- 1/4 cup cocoa powder
- 1/4 teaspoon salt
- 1/2 cup chopped hazelnuts
- Cooking spray

Instructions:

1. Prepare the Brownie Batter: In a mixing bowl, combine the melted butter, granulated sugar, and brown sugar. Whisk in the eggs and vanilla extract until smooth. In a separate bowl, whisk together the flour, cocoa powder, and salt. Gradually mix the dry ingredients into the wet ingredients until just combined. Fold in the chopped hazelnuts.
2. Preheat the Air Fryer: Set your air fryer to 320°F (160°C) and preheat for about 3 minutes.
3. Prepare the Mold: Lightly spray a silicone brownie mold with cooking spray. Divide the brownie batter evenly among the mold compartments.
4. Cook the Brownies: Place the silicone mold in the air fryer basket. Air fry at 320°F (160°C) for 12-15 minutes, or until a toothpick inserted in the center comes out mostly clean.
5. Cool and Serve: Allow the brownies to cool completely in the mold. Once cooled, remove the brownie cubes from the mold.

NUTRITIONAL DATA: CALORIES: 210 | PROTEIN: 3G | CARBOHYDRATES: 25G | FAT: 12G | FIBER: 2G | SUGAR: 18G | SODIUM: 80MG

Blueberry Crumble Muffins

PREPARATION TIME: 15 MINUTES | COOKING TIME: 15 MINUTES | PORTION SIZE: 12 MUFFINS

Ingredients:

For the Muffins:

- 1 1/2 cups all-purpose flour
- 1/2 cup granulated sugar
- 1/2 teaspoon salt
- 2 teaspoons baking powder
- 1/3 cup vegetable oil
- 1 large egg
- 1/3 cup milk
- 1 teaspoon vanilla extract
- 1 cup fresh or frozen blueberries

For the Crumble Topping:

- 1/2 cup all-purpose flour
- 1/4 cup granulated sugar
- 1/4 cup brown sugar
- 1/4 cup unsalted butter, melted
- 1/2 teaspoon ground cinnamon

Instructions:

1. Preheat the Air Fryer: Preheat your air fryer to 350°F (175°C) for about 3 minutes.
2. Prepare the Muffin Batter: In a large bowl, whisk together the flour, sugar, salt, and baking powder. In a separate bowl, mix the vegetable oil, egg, milk, and vanilla extract. Pour the wet ingredients into the dry ingredients and stir until just combined. Gently fold in the blueberries.
3. Prepare the Crumble Topping: In a small bowl, mix together the flour, granulated sugar, brown sugar, cinnamon, and melted butter until crumbly.
4. Assemble the Muffins: Line your air fryer basket with silicone muffin cups or use parchment paper liners. Fill each cup with the muffin batter about 3/4 full. Sprinkle the crumble topping generously over each muffin.
5. Air Fry the Muffins: Place the muffins in the air fryer basket in a single layer. Air fry at 350°F (175°C) for 12-15 minutes, or until a toothpick inserted into the center comes out clean.
6. Serve: Allow the muffins to cool slightly before serving. Enjoy them warm or at room temperature.

NUTRITIONAL DATA: CALORIES: 220 | PROTEIN: 3G | CARBOHYDRATES: 32G | FAT: 10G | FIBER: 1G | SUGAR: 18G | SODIUM: 180MG

Desserts

Air Fryer Cinnamon Sugar Donuts

PREPARATION TIME: 15 MINUTES I COOKING TIME: 10 MINUTES I PORTION SIZE: 8 DONUTS

Ingredients:

- 1 can (8 pieces) refrigerated biscuit dough
- 1/4 cup melted butter
- 1/2 cup granulated sugar
- 1 teaspoon ground cinnamon
- Cooking spray

Instructions:

1. Preheat the Air Fryer: Set your air fryer to 350°F (175°C) and preheat for about 3 minutes.
2. Prepare the Dough: Use a small round cutter or the cap of a bottle to cut out the centers of the biscuit dough pieces, creating donut shapes.
3. Air Fry the Donuts: Lightly spray the air fryer basket with cooking spray. Place the donuts in the basket in a single layer, leaving space between them. Air fry for 5-6 minutes, flipping halfway through, until they are golden brown.
4. Coat with Cinnamon Sugar: While the donuts are air frying, mix the sugar and cinnamon in a bowl. Once the donuts are cooked, brush them with melted butter and immediately toss them in the cinnamon sugar mixture to coat evenly.
5. Serve: Enjoy the donuts warm, either plain or with a dip of your choice.

NUTRITIONAL DATA: CALORIES: 220 | PROTEIN: 3G | CARBOHYDRATES: 26G | FAT: 12G | FIBER: 1G | SUGAR: 10G | SODIUM: 380MG

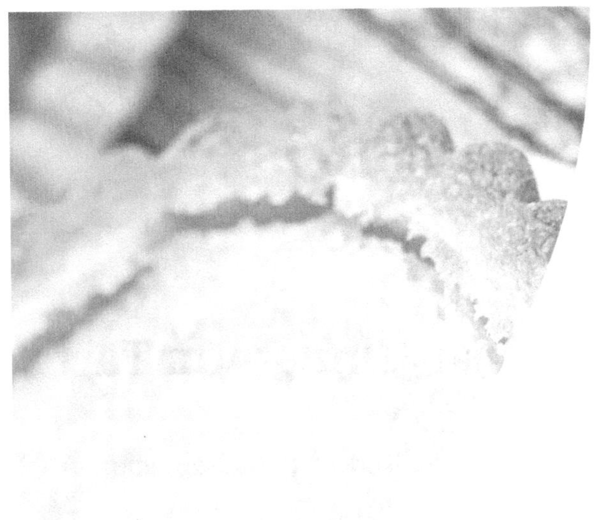

Lemon Ricotta Tarts

PREPARATION TIME: 20 MINUTES | COOKING TIME: 15 MINUTES | PORTION SIZE: 6 TARTS

Ingredients:

- 1 cup ricotta cheese
- 1/4 cup granulated sugar
- 2 large eggs
- 1/4 cup fresh lemon juice
- 1 tablespoon lemon zest
- 1 teaspoon vanilla extract
- 1 sheet puff pastry, thawed
- Powdered sugar, for dusting

Instructions:

1. Preheat the Air Fryer: Set your air fryer to 350°F (175°C) and preheat for about 3 minutes.
2. Prepare the Filling: In a medium bowl, whisk together the ricotta cheese, sugar, eggs, lemon juice, lemon zest, and vanilla extract until smooth and creamy.
3. Prepare the Pastry: Roll out the puff pastry sheet on a lightly floured surface. Cut it into 6 equal squares and press each square into an air fryer-safe tart mold, trimming any excess dough.
4. Assemble the Tarts: Spoon the lemon ricotta mixture evenly into each pastry-lined tart mold.
5. Cook the Tarts: Place the filled tart molds in the air fryer basket. Air fry at 350°F (175°C) for 12-15 minutes, or until the filling is set and the pastry is golden brown.
6. Serve: Allow the tarts to cool slightly before removing them from the molds. Dust with powdered sugar before serving.

NUTRITIONAL DATA: CALORIES: 220 | PROTEIN: 7G | CARBOHYDRATES: 22G | FAT: 12G | FIBER: 1G | SUGAR: 12G | SODIUM: 150MG

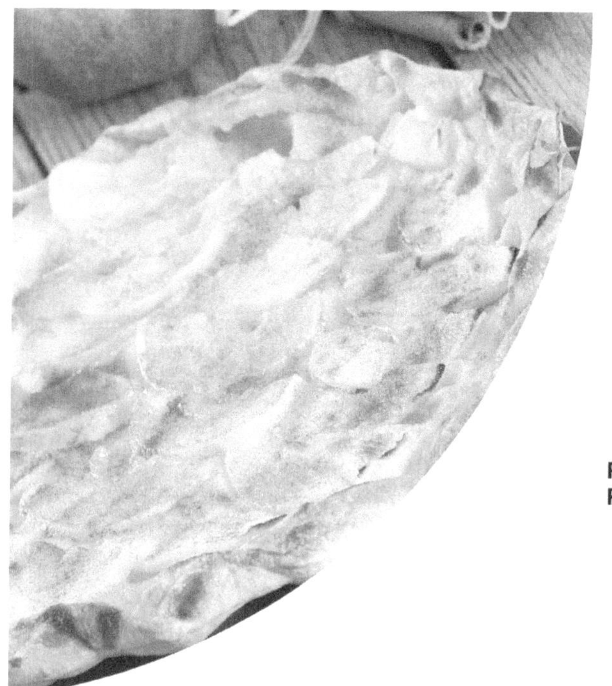

Pear Cinnamon Tart

PREPARATION TIME: 15 MINUTES I COOKING TIME: 20 MINUTES I PORTION SIZE: 6 SERVINGS

Ingredients:

- 1 sheet puff pastry, thawed
- 2 ripe pears, thinly sliced
- 2 tablespoons granulated sugar
- 1 teaspoon ground cinnamon
- 1 tablespoon lemon juice
- 1/4 cup almond flour (optional, for added texture)
- 1 egg, beaten (for egg wash)
- Powdered sugar (for dusting, optional)
- Cooking spray

Instructions:

1. Preheat the Air Fryer: Set your air fryer to 350°F (175°C) and preheat for about 3 minutes.
2. Prepare the Pears: In a bowl, toss the pear slices with lemon juice, sugar, and cinnamon until well coated.
3. Assemble the Tart: Roll out the puff pastry on a lightly floured surface and cut it into a circle or rectangle to fit your air fryer basket. Sprinkle the almond flour evenly over the puff pastry. Arrange the pear slices on top of the almond flour in an overlapping pattern. Brush the edges of the puff pastry with the beaten egg.
4. Cook the Tart: Lightly spray the air fryer basket with cooking spray. Carefully transfer the assembled tart into the basket. Air fry for 15-20 minutes, or until the pastry is golden brown and puffed up, and the pears are tender.
5. Serve: Allow the tart to cool slightly before dusting with powdered sugar, if desired. Serve warm.

NUTRITIONAL DATA: CALORIES: 240 | PROTEIN: 4G | CARBOHYDRATES: 28G | FAT: 13G | FIBER: 3G | SUGAR: 12G | SODIUM: 150MG

Desserts

Chocolate Biscuits

PREPARATION TIME: 15 MINUTES I COOKING TIME: 10 MINUTES I PORTION SIZE: 12 BISCUITS

Ingredients:

- 1 cup all-purpose flour
- 1/4 cup cocoa powder
- 1/2 teaspoon baking powder
- 1/4 teaspoon baking soda
- 1/4 teaspoon salt
- 1/2 cup unsalted butter, softened
- 1/2 cup granulated sugar
- 1/4 cup brown sugar
- 1 large egg
- 1 teaspoon vanilla extract
- 1/2 cup chocolate chips (optional)

Instructions:

1. Preheat the Air Fryer: Set your air fryer to 350°F (175°C) and preheat for about 3 minutes.
2. Prepare the Dough: In a medium bowl, whisk together the flour, cocoa powder, baking powder, baking soda, and salt. In a separate large bowl, cream together the softened butter, granulated sugar, and brown sugar until light and fluffy. Beat in the egg and vanilla extract until well combined. Gradually mix in the dry ingredients until a dough forms. Stir in the chocolate chips if using.
3. Shape the Biscuits: Roll the dough into 12 equal balls and flatten them slightly to form biscuits. Place the biscuits in an air fryer-safe mold or directly into the air fryer basket, leaving space between each one.
4. Cook the Biscuits: Air fry at 350°F (175°C) for 8-10 minutes, or until the biscuits are set and slightly firm to the touch.
5. Serve: Allow the biscuits to cool on a wire rack before serving. Enjoy warm or at room temperature.

NUTRITIONAL DATA: CALORIES: 160 | PROTEIN: 2G | CARBOHYDRATES: 22G | FAT: 8G | FIBER: 1G | SUGAR: 12G | SODIUM: 120MG

Apple Pies from Hot Air Fryer

PREPARATION TIME: 20 MINUTES I COOKING TIME: 15 MINUTES I PORTION SIZE: 4 MINI PIES

Ingredients:

- 2 medium apples, peeled, cored, and diced
- 1/4 cup granulated sugar
- 1 teaspoon cinnamon
- 1 tablespoon lemon juice
- 1 tablespoon butter, melted
- 1 sheet puff pastry, thawed
- 1 egg, beaten (for egg wash)
- Powdered sugar, for dusting (optional)

Instructions:

1. Preheat the Air Fryer: Set your air fryer to 350°F (175°C) and preheat for about 3 minutes.
2. Prepare the Apple Filling: In a medium bowl, mix the diced apples with granulated sugar, cinnamon, lemon juice, and melted butter. Stir until the apples are evenly coated.
3. Prepare the Puff Pastry: Roll out the puff pastry sheet on a lightly floured surface. Cut the pastry into 8 equal squares.
4. Place in Molds: Lightly spray air fryer-safe tart molds with cooking spray. Press each pastry square into the molds, ensuring the dough covers the bottom and sides.
5. Assemble the Pies: Spoon the apple filling evenly into each pastry-lined mold. Fold any excess pastry over the top of the filling.
6. Brush with Egg Wash: Lightly brush the tops of each pie with the beaten egg for a golden finish.
7. Cook the Pies: Place the filled molds in the air fryer basket, leaving space between each one. Air fry at 350°F (175°C) for 12-15 minutes, or until the pies are golden brown and crispy.
8. Serve: Let the pies cool slightly before removing them from the molds. Dust with powdered sugar before serving if desired.

NUTRITIONAL DATA: CALORIES: 220 | PROTEIN: 3G | CARBOHYDRATES: 29G | FAT: 12G | FIBER: 2G | SUGAR: 14G | SODIUM: 170MG

Desserts

Banana Cake with Chocolate Chips

PREPARATION TIME: 15 MINUTES | COOKING TIME: 20 MINUTES | PORTION SIZE: 8 SERVINGS

Ingredients:

- 1 cup all-purpose flour
- 1/2 teaspoon baking soda
- 1/4 teaspoon salt
- 1/4 cup unsalted butter, softened
- 1/2 cup granulated sugar
- 1 large egg
- 1/2 teaspoon vanilla extract
- 2 ripe bananas, mashed
- 1/2 cup chocolate chips
- Cooking spray

Instructions:

1. Preheat the Air Fryer: Set your air fryer to 320°F (160°C) and preheat for about 3 minutes.
2. Prepare the Dry Ingredients: In a medium bowl, whisk together the flour, baking soda, and salt. Set aside.
3. Cream the Butter and Sugar: In a separate large bowl, cream the softened butter and sugar until light and fluffy. Beat in the egg and vanilla extract until well combined.
4. Mix the Wet Ingredients: Add the mashed bananas to the butter mixture and stir until combined.
5. Combine and Add Chocolate Chips: Gradually add the dry ingredients to the wet ingredients, mixing until just combined. Fold in the chocolate chips.
6. Prepare the Cake Mold: Lightly spray an air fryer-safe cake mold with cooking spray. Pour the batter into the mold, smoothing the top.
7. Cook the Cake: Place the mold in the air fryer basket and cook at 320°F (160°C) for 18-20 minutes, or until a toothpick inserted into the center comes out clean.
8. Cool and Serve: Allow the cake to cool in the mold before removing. Slice and serve warm or at room temperature.

NUTRITIONAL DATA: CALORIES: 230 | PROTEIN: 3G | CARBOHYDRATES: 35G | FAT: 10G | FIBER: 2G | SUGAR: 20G | SODIUM: 150MG

Raspberry Tarts

PREPARATION TIME: 15 MINUTES I COOKING TIME: 12 MINUTES I PORTION SIZE: 6 TARTS

Ingredients:

- 1 sheet puff pastry, thawed
- 1/2 cup raspberry jam
- 1 cup fresh raspberries
- 1/4 cup granulated sugar
- 1 tablespoon cornstarch
- 1 tablespoon lemon juice
- Powdered sugar, for dusting

Instructions:

1. Preheat the Air Fryer: Set your air fryer to 350°F (175°C) and preheat for about 3 minutes.
2. Prepare the Puff Pastry: Roll out the puff pastry sheet on a lightly floured surface. Cut the pastry into 6 equal squares.
3. Place in Molds: Press each square of puff pastry into individual air fryer-safe tart molds, ensuring the pastry covers the bottom and sides of the molds.
4. Prepare the Raspberry Filling: In a small bowl, mix together the raspberry jam, fresh raspberries, granulated sugar, cornstarch, and lemon juice until the raspberries are evenly coated.
5. Assemble the Tarts: Spoon the raspberry filling into each pastry-lined mold, distributing it evenly among the six tarts.
6. Cook the Tarts: Place the filled molds in the air fryer basket. Air fry at 350°F (175°C) for 10-12 minutes, or until the pastry is golden brown and the filling is bubbly.
7. Serve: Allow the tarts to cool slightly in the molds before removing them. Dust with powdered sugar before serving.

NUTRITIONAL DATA: CALORIES: 220 | PROTEIN: 3G | CARBOHYDRATES: 30G | FAT: 10G | FIBER: 2G | SUGAR: 18G | SODIUM: 150MG

Chapter 7: Bread

Here, you'll learn how versatile and efficient your air fryer can be for baking various types of bread. From classic loaves to creative and flavorful rolls, these recipes are designed to help you bake delicious bread with minimal effort and time.

Using the air fryer, you can achieve perfect bread with a crisp crust and soft interior, all while using less energy and avoiding the need to preheat a traditional oven. Whether you're new to baking or an experienced baker, you'll find these recipes easy to follow and highly rewarding.

Enjoy the convenience of baking fresh, homemade bread in your air fryer. Each recipe is crafted to ensure great results every time, making your kitchen endeavors both fun and successful. Let's dive in and start baking bread that your whole family will love!

Airy Potato Bread
Whole Wheat Bread with Nuts and Seeds
Olive Spelt Bread
Roasted Onion Bread
Herb Bread with Garlic Butter
Whole Spelt Bread
Pumpkin Seed Baguette
Olive Rosemary Flatbread
Potato Herb Bread
Sweet Potato Cinnamon Bread

Bread

Airy Potato Bread

PREPARATION TIME: 20 MINUTES I COOKING TIME: 35 MINUTES I PORTION SIZE: 1 LOAF (10-12 SLICES)

Ingredients:

- 2 cups all-purpose flour
- 1 teaspoon salt
- 1 teaspoon sugar
- 1 teaspoon active dry yeast
- 1/2 cup mashed potatoes (cooked and cooled)
- 3/4 cup warm water
- 2 tablespoons olive oil
- 1 tablespoon fresh rosemary, chopped (optional)

Instructions:

1. Preheat the Air Fryer: Set your air fryer to 350°F (175°C) and preheat for about 3 minutes.
2. Mix the Dough: In a large bowl, combine the flour, salt, sugar, and yeast. Add the mashed potatoes, warm water, and olive oil. Mix until a soft dough forms.
3. Knead the Dough: Transfer the dough to a lightly floured surface and knead for about 5 minutes, until smooth and elastic. If using, knead in the chopped rosemary.
4. First Rise: Place the dough in a lightly oiled bowl, cover with a damp cloth, and let it rise in a warm place for about 1 hour, or until doubled in size.
5. Shape the Dough: Once the dough has risen, punch it down and shape it into a loaf. Place the loaf in a greased air fryer-safe bread pan.
6. Second Rise: Let the dough rise in the pan for another 30 minutes.
7. Cook the Bread: Place the bread pan in the air fryer basket. Air fry at 350°F (175°C) for 30-35 minutes, or until the bread is golden brown and sounds hollow when tapped.
8. Cool and Serve: Allow the bread to cool in the pan for a few minutes before transferring it to a wire rack to cool completely. Slice and enjoy.

NUTRITIONAL DATA: CALORIES: 180 | PROTEIN: 4G | CARBOHYDRATES: 32G | FAT: 4G | FIBER: 2G | SUGAR: 1G | SODIUM: 230MG

Whole Wheat Bread with Nuts and Seeds

PREPARATION TIME: 15 MINUTES I COOKING TIME: 25 MINUTES I PORTION SIZE: 1 LOAF (10-12 SLICES)

Ingredients:

- 2 cups whole wheat flour
- 1/2 cup mixed nuts (such as walnuts, almonds), chopped
- 1/4 cup mixed seeds (such as sunflower, flax, and sesame)
- 1 packet (7g) instant yeast
- 1 teaspoon salt
- 1 tablespoon honey
- 1 tablespoon olive oil
- 1 cup warm water
- 1 tablespoon oats (optional, for topping)

Instructions:

1. Preheat the Air Fryer: Set your air fryer to 350°F (175°C) and preheat for about 3 minutes.
2. Prepare the Dough: In a large mixing bowl, combine the whole wheat flour, chopped nuts, mixed seeds, instant yeast, and salt. Stir in the honey, olive oil, and warm water. Mix until a soft dough forms.
3. Knead the Dough: On a lightly floured surface, knead the dough for about 5 minutes until smooth and elastic. Form the dough into a loaf shape.
4. Place in a Mold: Lightly grease an air fryer-safe loaf mold. Place the dough in the mold, cover with a clean cloth, and let it rise in a warm place for about 30 minutes, or until doubled in size.
5. Cook the Bread: Once the dough has risen, place the loaf mold in the air fryer basket. If desired, sprinkle the top with oats. Air fry at 350°F (175°C) for 25 minutes, or until the bread is golden brown and sounds hollow when tapped on the bottom.
6. Cool and Serve: Remove the bread from the mold and let it cool on a wire rack before slicing.

NUTRITIONAL DATA: CALORIES: 180 | PROTEIN: 5G | CARBOHYDRATES: 28G | FAT: 7G | FIBER: 4G | SUGAR: 3G | SODIUM: 180MG

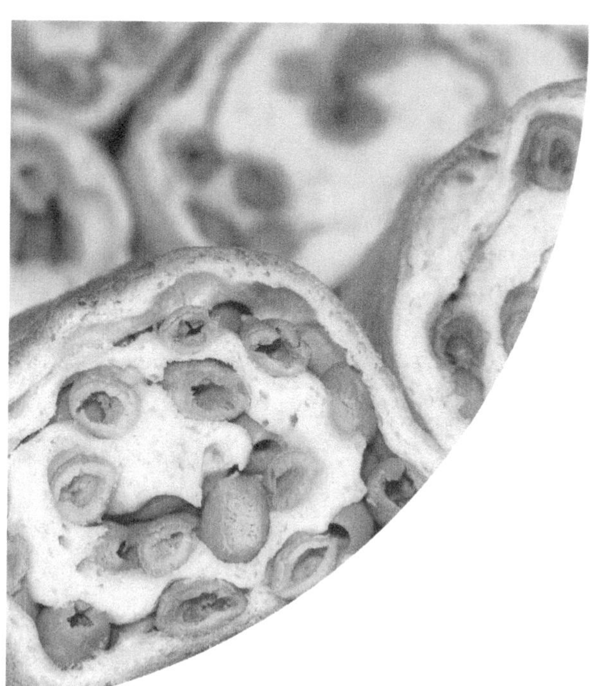

Bread

Olive Spelt Bread

PREPARATION TIME: 20 MINUTES I COOKING TIME: 25 MINUTES I PORTION SIZE: 1 LOAF (10-12 SLICES)

Ingredients:

- 2 cups spelt flour
- 1/2 cup whole wheat flour
- 1/2 cup pitted black olives, chopped
- 1 packet (7g) instant yeast
- 1 teaspoon salt
- 1 tablespoon olive oil
- 1 tablespoon honey or maple syrup
- 1 cup warm water
- 1 tablespoon fresh rosemary, chopped (optional)

Instructions:

1. Preheat the Air Fryer: Set your air fryer to 350°F (175°C) and preheat for about 3 minutes.
2. Prepare the Dough: In a large mixing bowl, combine the spelt flour, whole wheat flour, chopped olives, instant yeast, and salt. Stir in the olive oil, honey or maple syrup, and warm water. Mix until a soft dough forms.
3. Knead the Dough: On a lightly floured surface, knead the dough for about 5 minutes until smooth and elastic. If using, knead in the fresh rosemary during this step. Form the dough into a loaf shape.
4. Place in a Mold: Lightly grease an air fryer-safe loaf mold. Place the dough in the mold, cover with a clean cloth, and let it rise in a warm place for about 30 minutes, or until doubled in size.
5. Cook the Bread: Once the dough has risen, place the loaf mold in the air fryer basket. Air fry at 350°F (175°C) for 25 minutes, or until the bread is golden brown and sounds hollow when tapped on the bottom.
6. Cool and Serve: Remove the bread from the mold and let it cool on a wire rack before slicing.

NUTRITIONAL DATA: CALORIES: 190 | PROTEIN: 5G | CARBOHYDRATES: 30G | FAT: 6G | FIBER: 4G | SUGAR: 2G | SODIUM: 200MG

Roasted Onion Bread

PREPARATION TIME: 20 MINUTES I COOKING TIME: 25 MINUTES I PORTION SIZE: 1 LOAF (10-12 SLICES)

Ingredients:

- 2 cups all-purpose flour
- 1/2 cup whole wheat flour
- 1 packet (7g) instant yeast
- 1 teaspoon salt
- 1 tablespoon sugar
- 1 large onion, finely chopped
- 2 tablespoons olive oil (divided)
- 1 cup warm water
- 1/2 teaspoon dried thyme (optional)

Instructions:

1. Preheat the Air Fryer: Set your air fryer to 350°F (175°C) and preheat for about 3 minutes.
2. Roast the Onions: Heat 1 tablespoon of olive oil in a pan over medium heat. Add the chopped onions and sauté until they are golden brown and caramelized, about 8-10 minutes. Set aside to cool slightly.
3. Prepare the Dough: In a large mixing bowl, combine the all-purpose flour, whole wheat flour, instant yeast, salt, sugar, and dried thyme if using. Stir in the roasted onions and the remaining 1 tablespoon of olive oil. Gradually add the warm water, mixing until a soft dough forms.
4. Knead the Dough: On a lightly floured surface, knead the dough for about 5 minutes until smooth and elastic. Form the dough into a loaf shape.
5. Place in a Mold: Lightly grease an air fryer-safe loaf mold. Place the dough in the mold, cover with a clean cloth, and let it rise in a warm place for about 30 minutes, or until doubled in size.
6. Cook the Bread: Once the dough has risen, place the loaf mold in the air fryer basket. Air fry at 350°F (175°C) for 20-25 minutes, or until the bread is golden brown and sounds hollow when tapped on the bottom.
7. Cool and Serve: Remove the bread from the mold and let it cool on a wire rack before slicing.

NUTRITIONAL DATA: CALORIES: 210 | PROTEIN: 5G | CARBOHYDRATES: 35G | FAT: 5G | FIBER: 3G | SUGAR: 3G | SODIUM: 250MG

Herb Bread with Garlic Butter

PREPARATION TIME: 20 MINUTES I COOKING TIME: 25 MINUTES I PORTION SIZE: 1 LOAF (10-12 SLICES)

Ingredients:

- 2 cups all-purpose flour
- 1/2 cup whole wheat flour
- 1 packet (7g) instant yeast
- 1 teaspoon salt
- 1 tablespoon sugar
- 1/4 cup fresh herbs (such as parsley, thyme, rosemary), chopped
- 3 tablespoons garlic butter, softened
- 1 tablespoon olive oil
- 1 cup warm water

Instructions:

1. Preheat the Air Fryer: Set your air fryer to 350°F (175°C) and preheat for about 3 minutes.
2. Prepare the Dough: In a large mixing bowl, combine the all-purpose flour, whole wheat flour, instant yeast, salt, sugar, and chopped herbs. Stir in the olive oil and warm water. Mix until a soft dough forms.
3. Knead the Dough: Transfer the dough to a lightly floured surface and knead for about 5 minutes until smooth and elastic.
4. First Rise: Place the dough in a lightly greased bowl, cover with a clean cloth, and let it rise in a warm place for about 1 hour, or until doubled in size.
5. Shape and Second Rise: After the first rise, punch down the dough and shape it into a loaf. Place the loaf in an air fryer-safe mold, cover, and let it rise for another 30 minutes.
6. Cook the Bread: Place the mold in the air fryer basket. Air fry at 350°F (175°C) for 25-30 minutes, or until the bread is golden brown and sounds hollow when tapped on the bottom.
7. Cool and Serve: Remove the bread from the mold and let it cool on a wire rack before slicing. Serve with additional garlic butter if desired.

NUTRITIONAL DATA: CALORIES: 210 | PROTEIN: 5G | CARBOHYDRATES: 35G | FAT: 5G | FIBER: 3G | SUGAR: 3G | SODIUM: 250MG

Bread

Whole Spelt Bread

PREPARATION TIME: 20 MINUTES | COOKING TIME: 25-30 MINUTES | PORTION SIZE: 1 LOAF (10-12 SLICES)

Ingredients:

- 3 cups whole spelt flour
- 1 1/2 teaspoons salt
- 1 packet (7g) instant yeast
- 1 tablespoon honey or maple syrup
- 1 1/4 cups warm water
- 1 tablespoon olive oil
- Optional: Seeds for topping (e.g., sunflower seeds, flaxseeds)

Instructions:

1. Preheat the Air Fryer: Set your air fryer to 350°F (175°C) and preheat for about 3 minutes.
2. Prepare the Dough: In a large mixing bowl, combine the whole spelt flour, salt, and instant yeast. Stir in the honey or maple syrup and warm water. Mix until a soft dough forms.
3. Knead the Dough: Transfer the dough to a lightly floured surface and knead for about 5 minutes until smooth and elastic.
4. First Rise: Place the dough in a lightly greased bowl, cover with a clean cloth, and let it rise in a warm place for about 1 hour, or until doubled in size.
5. Shape and Second Rise: After the first rise, punch down the dough and shape it into a loaf. Place the loaf in an air fryer-safe mol, cover, and let it rise for another 30 minutes.
6. Cook the Bread: Place the mold with the dough in the air fryer basket. Air fry at 350°F (175°C) for 25-30 minutes, or until the bread is golden brown and sounds hollow when tapped on the bottom.
7. Cool and Serve: Remove the bread from the mold and let it cool on a wire rack before slicing.

NUTRITIONAL DATA: CALORIES: 190 | PROTEIN: 5G | CARBOHYDRATES: 34G | FAT: 3G | FIBER: 5G | SUGAR: 3G | SODIUM: 250MG

Bread

Pumpkin Seed Baguette

PREPARATION TIME: 20 MINUTES I COOKING TIME: 25 MINUTES I PORTION SIZE: 1 BAGUETTE (10-12 SLICES)

Ingredients:

- 2 cups bread flour
- 1/2 cup whole wheat flour
- 1/4 cup pumpkin seeds, plus extra for topping
- 1 packet (7g) instant yeast
- 1 teaspoon salt
- 1 teaspoon sugar
- 1 cup warm water
- 1 tablespoon olive oil

Instructions:

1. Preheat the Air Fryer: Set your air fryer to 350°F (175°C) and preheat for about 3 minutes.
2. Prepare the Dough: In a large mixing bowl, combine the bread flour, whole wheat flour, pumpkin seeds, instant yeast, salt, and sugar. Stir in the warm water and olive oil, mixing until a soft dough forms.
3. Knead the Dough: Transfer the dough to a lightly floured surface and knead for about 5-7 minutes until smooth and elastic.
4. First Rise: Place the dough in a lightly greased bowl, cover with a clean cloth, and let it rise in a warm place for about 1 hour, or until doubled in size.
5. Shape the Baguette: After the first rise, punch down the dough and shape it into a baguette. Place the baguette on a piece of parchment paper that fits your air fryer basket. Cover and let it rise for another 30 minutes.
6. Top and Cook the Baguette: Brush the top of the baguette with a little water and sprinkle extra pumpkin seeds on top. Place the baguette in the air fryer basket. Air fry at 350°F (175°C) for 20-25 minutes, or until the baguette is golden brown and sounds hollow when tapped on the bottom.
7. Cool and Serve: Remove the baguette from the air fryer and let it cool on a wire rack before slicing.

NUTRITIONAL DATA: CALORIES: 200 | PROTEIN: 6G | CARBOHYDRATES: 34G | FAT: 5G | FIBER: 3G | SUGAR: 1G | SODIUM: 250MG

Olive Rosemary Flatbread

PREPARATION TIME: 15 MINUTES I COOKING TIME: 15 MINUTES I PORTION SIZE: 8 SLICES

Ingredients:

- 2 cups all-purpose flour
- 1 teaspoon salt
- 1 teaspoon sugar
- 1 packet (7g) instant yeast
- 1/2 cup warm water
- 1/4 cup olive oil
- 1/2 cup pitted olives, sliced
- 1 tablespoon fresh rosemary, chopped
- 1 tablespoon olive oil (for brushing)
- Coarse sea salt, for sprinkling

Instructions:

1. Preheat the Air Fryer: Set your air fryer to 375°F (190°C) and preheat for about 3 minutes.
2. Prepare the Dough: In a large mixing bowl, combine the flour, salt, sugar, and instant yeast. Stir in the warm water and olive oil, mixing until a soft dough forms.
3. Knead the Dough: Transfer the dough to a lightly floured surface and knead for about 5 minutes until smooth and elastic.
4. First Rise: Place the dough in a lightly greased bowl, cover with a clean cloth, and let it rise in a warm place for about 30 minutes, or until slightly puffed.
5. Shape the Flatbread: After the first rise, punch down the dough and shape it into a flatbread on a piece of parchment paper that fits your air fryer basket. Press the sliced olives and chopped rosemary into the surface of the dough. Brush the top with olive oil and sprinkle with coarse sea salt.
6. Cook the Flatbread: Place the flatbread in the air fryer basket. Air fry at 375°F (190°C) for 12-15 minutes, or until the flatbread is golden brown and crispy.
7. Cool and Serve: Remove the flatbread from the air fryer and let it cool slightly before slicing.

NUTRITIONAL DATA: CALORIES: 180 | PROTEIN: 4G | CARBOHYDRATES: 22G | FAT: 8G | FIBER: 2G | SUGAR: 1G | SODIUM: 200MG

Bread

Potato Herb Bread

PREPARATION TIME: 15 MINUTES I COOKING TIME: 25-30 MINUTES I PORTION SIZE: 1 LOAF (10-12 SLICES)

Ingredients:

- 2 cups all-purpose flour
- 1 tablespoon baking powder
- 1/2 teaspoon baking soda
- 1/2 teaspoon salt
- 1 teaspoon dried thyme
- 1 teaspoon dried rosemary
- 1 cup mashed potatoes
- 1/2 cup buttermilk
- 1/4 cup olive oil
- 1 large egg
- 1 tablespoon honey
- 1/4 cup chopped chives

Instructions:

1. Preheat the Air Fryer: Set your air fryer to 350°F (175°C) and preheat for about 3 minutes.
2. Prepare the Dry Ingredients: In a large bowl, whisk together the flour, baking powder, baking soda, salt, dried thyme, and dried rosemary.
3. Mix the Wet Ingredients: In a separate bowl, combine the mashed potatoes, buttermilk, olive oil, egg, and honey. Stir until smooth.
4. Combine and Mix: Gradually add the dry ingredients to the wet ingredients, mixing just until combined. Stir in the chopped chives.
5. Prepare the Bread Mold: Grease an air fryer-safe mold or line it with parchment paper. Pour the batter into the prepared mold, spreading it evenly.
6. Cook the Bread: Place the mold in the air fryer basket. Air fry at 350°F (175°C) for 25-30 minutes, or until a toothpick inserted into the center comes out clean.
7. Cool and Serve: Allow the bread to cool in the mold for a few minutes before transferring it to a wire rack to cool completely. Slice and serve.

NUTRITIONAL DATA: CALORIES: 180 | PROTEIN: 4G | CARBOHYDRATES: 32G | FAT: 4G | FIBER: 2G | SUGAR: 1G | SODIUM: 230MG

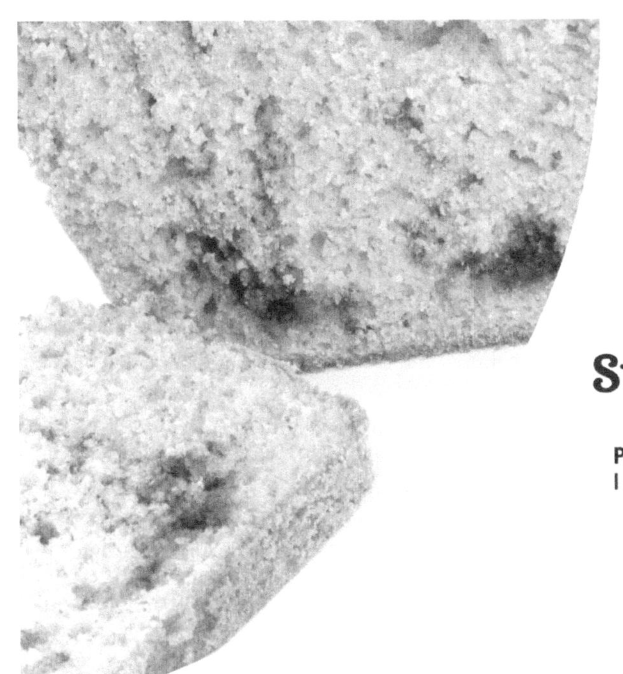

Sweet Potato Cinnamon Bread

PREPARATION TIME: 15 MINUTES | COOKING TIME: 25-30 MINUTES | PORTION SIZE: 1 LOAF (10-12 SLICES)

Ingredients:

- 1 1/2 cups all-purpose flour
- 1 teaspoon baking powder
- 1/2 teaspoon baking soda
- 1 teaspoon ground cinnamon
- 1/2 teaspoon ground nutmeg
- 1/4 teaspoon salt
- 1 cup mashed sweet potato
- 1/2 cup granulated sugar
- 1/4 cup brown sugar
- 1/2 cup melted butter
- 2 large eggs
- 1 teaspoon vanilla extract
- 1/2 cup milk

Instructions:

1. Preheat the Air Fryer: Set your air fryer to 350°F (175°C) and preheat for about 3 minutes.
2. Prepare the Dry Ingredients: In a medium bowl, whisk together the flour, baking powder, baking soda, cinnamon, nutmeg, and salt.
3. Mix the Wet Ingredients: In a separate large bowl, combine the mashed sweet potato, sugar, brown sugar, melted butter, eggs, vanilla extract, and milk. Mix until smooth.
4. Combine and Mix: Gradually add the dry ingredients to the wet ingredients, stirring just until combined.
5. Prepare the Bread Mold: Grease an air fryer-safe mold or line it with parchment paper. Pour the batter into the prepared mold, spreading it evenly.
6. Cook the Bread: Place the mold in the air fryer basket. Air fry at 350°F (175°C) for 25-30 minutes, or until a toothpick inserted into the center comes out clean.
7. Cool and Serve: Allow the bread to cool in the mold for a few minutes before transferring it to a wire rack to cool completely. Slice and serve.

NUTRITIONAL DATA: CALORIES: 220 | PROTEIN: 4G | CARBOHYDRATES: 32G | FAT: 9G | FIBER: 2G | SUGAR: 15G | SODIUM: 180MG

Conclusion: Experimenting and Adapting

In this journey through the world of beginner air fryer recipes, we have explored a wide range of delicious and creative dishes. From classics like french fries to fish, meat, and vegetable dishes, we've learned how to make the most of this versatile appliance.

One of the best aspects of cooking is the freedom to experiment and adapt recipes to our personal preferences. We've learned to play with ingredients, adjust temperatures, and cooking times to achieve increasingly personalized and satisfying results. The air fryer is a fantastic tool that allows us to prepare delicious meals in a healthier and more convenient way, and with a bit of creativity, we can truly unleash our culinary imagination.

- **Further Ideas and Inspiration**

Our exploration of beginner air fryer recipes is just the beginning of the culinary journey. There are many more recipes to try, techniques to perfect, and dishes to discover. Here are some additional ideas and inspiration to continue your journey:

- **Explore World Cuisines:** Try traditional recipes from different culinary cultures and discover new flavors and aromas that will surprise you.
- **Experiment with Ingredients:** Don't be afraid to step out of your comfort zone and try new and unusual ingredients. You might discover new favorite dishes!
- **Share Your Creations:** Invite friends and family to enjoy the dishes prepared with your air fryer and share your recipes and tricks with the online community. Sharing culinary experiences is a great way to connect and learn from others.

Always remember to have fun in the kitchen and not take yourself too seriously. Cooking should be an enjoyable and rewarding experience, so relax, have fun, and enjoy the culinary journey!

With this in mind, I wish you much joy and success on your culinary journey with your air fryer. May every meal be an opportunity to experiment, learn, and share valuable moments with the people you love.

Acknowledgements

I want to express my deepest gratitude to everyone who made the creation of this book, "Air Fryer Cookbook for Beginners: Quick and Easy Preparations for Healthy Meals," possible. It has been an incredible journey to share my passion for cooking and discover the benefits of the air fryer together.

To my family:
A special thank you to my husband and our two children. Your patience, love, and unwavering support have made this journey even more meaningful. Thank you for enthusiastically tasting every dish, enduring the long hours spent in the kitchen, and always believing in me. You are my inspiration and my strength.

To my friends:
A heartfelt thank you to my friends, who have always encouraged my culinary adventures. Thank you for your support, for the evenings spent trying new recipes, and for sharing your ideas and suggestions with me. Your friendship and enthusiasm have played a crucial role in the creation of this book.

A special thank you to the readers:
Thank you for your curiosity and desire to explore new culinary techniques. I hope that the recipes and tips in this book have inspired you to experiment and have fun in the kitchen, creating dishes that not only delight the palate but also promote a healthy lifestyle. Your support and passion for cooking are the driving forces that make this journey even more rewarding.
With gratitude,

Clara Müller

Don't Forget Your Free Bonus
Scan the QR Code Below

Or Copy and Paste the Link Below
https://lc.cx/R3NACA

Made in United States
Cleveland, OH
09 December 2024

11611029R00066